"I'm an engineer, and when I was in school, soft subjects like psychology and sociology never interested me much. If it wasn't math or science or something analytical, I pretty much avoided it. But I've learned through experience that getting along with people, understanding what motivates the people you work with, respecting them as equals, are the keys to getting things done efficiently. The relationships we develop with the people around us directly impact our effectiveness in getting our jobs done, and how much we accomplish as a whole. Frank and Susan help us loosen up and consider our relationships with coworkers, and how that could help us all improve."

Dwayne Intveld

Engineering Manager, Product Evaluation • John Deere Construction & Forestry Division

"Through their past careers and life experiences, Frank and Susan Pastizzo have gained a deep understanding of the importance of human relationships in the workplace and how simple behavior choices can turn a potential negative experience into a positive and meaningful one. Spend an hour with Frank and Sue in the pages of this book, and you'll walk away with advice and suggestions that will give a fresh new perspective on some simple personal changes you can make that will make every workday meaningful and fun."

Stewart Foster

Project Manager, IBM

"Attitude and free will - we all have choices throughout every day -choices to view things through a positive lens or a negative lens. I often hear people say "that person has such an attitude!" By saying only the word "attitude," it is immediately understood by most people that the person mentioned has a negative attitude. Today I am going to choose to view my world positively, not react to anything in an angry manner, and to try to understand others. After all, people aren't necessarily difficult, they are different. Frank and Susan's book affirms my belief."

Carl Petitto

OTR/L, CHCC, Owner, Adirondack Physical & Occupational Therapy, LLC

"**F**rank Pastizzo had something to say that touched each person's life and job situation. His presentation is hilarious and entertaining while still making his audiences think about how they work and interact with other people. Frank's seminar is truly captivating and motivating."

Tom Grove
President and CEO, Oregon Pacific Banking Company

"**H**umor and laughter have long been known to aid healing and promote health. It was not until Frank Pastizzo came along that we have been able to experience this healing through humor as health professionals. After all, isn't it, "Physician, heal thyself."? Frank's experiences as a health care worker and his knowledge of health care professionals enable him to accurately hit the funny bone of health care providers as they are both entertained and enlightened. Frank talks the health care professional's language. He teaches us that we are not alone in our reactions to pain, fear, suffering, joy, and the awe, that is health care. After spending time with Frank in his world and getting exposed to his obviously exuberant take on life and health care, we can all go back to our health care jobs renewed with more compassion... and a smile!"

Kim Byas, Sr., MPH
Regional Executive, American Hospital Association

"**F**rank Pastizzo's presentations have been extremely well received by employees at all levels of the school system. He has brought joy to many people and caused them to pause and think about important issues, while at the same time being genuinely and totally entertained!"

John P. O'Connor
Staff Development Supervisor, Loudoun County (Virginia) Public Schools

"**I**was in the audience at AuSable Valley Central School today. On my way out, I purchased your book and told you that your presentation was the BEST opening day presentation I had attended in nineteen years of teaching. I was serious. This afternoon, you demonstrated what we know about what kids (and adults) all need to learn. You showed us with your wit, your stories, and your music. You made us feel like we're a part of the whole, that we're in this together. I so enjoyed laughing and crying with you this afternoon. You can be sure that this is one opening day of a new school year that none of us will forget. I will carry your message of CHERISH with me throughout the year and into the years ahead. Thank you."

Sarah Smithson
Keeseville, NY Elementary School

"The vibrations rippling across campus here as the result of your presentations are tremendous, positive, and uplifting to say the least. Thanks again for being the right person with the right message at the right time in the right place!"

Randall J. VanWagoner, Ph.D.
President, Mohawk Valley Community College

"You both are what the fields of entertainment, presentation and education are all about. Merging comedy, music, education, community, suffering, sadness, family, happiness (too many to name) along with just a plain old sense of togetherness; it's exactly what businesses, colleges, high schools, hospitals and human service need in today's day and age."

Bill Dustin
President, The Central New York Showcase

"You are fantastic! After seeing you speak in New York, I knew you would be a smash at our national conference. You were! Thank you for your inspiring and laugh-filled message. You have wonderful energy!"

Tammara Geary
National Association of Persons in Supported Employment (APSE)

Warming Up The Workplace

by Frank and Susan Pastizzo
Warm Up The Workplace, Inc,

Layout/Design: Valisha Arnold and Mark Todd of Ailian Design
Design, Layout, and Illustrations Produced by:

Λ I L I Λ N
AILIAN DESIGN
PO Box 250, Norwood, NY 13668 • (315) 353-2222
w w w . c p s a v e r . c o m

 Pastizzo Presentations and
Warm Up The Workplace, Inc.

ISBN: 978-0-9718805-1-1

Printed in Canada

To Christina.

It's all human service. Keep it warm.

Susan Pastryp

Clara Pastryp

Contents

Contents Continued

Introduction

This is my job, it's not my life. If you believe this is true, then this book is for you. If you believe this is false, then this book is for you.

If you separate your attitudes and behaviors into *at work* and *life* categories, then we hope to illustrate how you may be missing out on a whole lot of good things, since you spend a large portion of your waking hours, and your energy, in a work setting. It makes sense that the values you want in your life should be present wherever you are living it.

If you believe that your behavior at work counts just as much as it counts when you are with friends and family, we hope these pages will encourage you to keep doing what you are doing, and perhaps even find ways to increase the number of positive actions you take to affect the quality of your days, and the days of those you live and work with.

We believe that all jobs are human service jobs. We work alongside people for the benefit of other people, no matter what we are doing. When we are working alone it is still usually for the benefit of others. When we are not at work, our actions are still in great part performed with other people's wants and needs in mind. Being aware of and employing "on purpose" behaviors to improve our human services both at work and in life in general—these are the reasons for putting together this book.

Note

These pages are made up of collected columns we have published individually over some years. They are not presented chronologically, but rather are organized into general themes. The point of view varies from first person, to other person, to third person and back again. They represent our attempt to share our ideas and learnings from both of our career fields, and from interacting with diverse organizations, schools, hospitals, factories, banks and other businesses around the country. We continue to write monthly columns and publish them on the web. They are free, and can be obtained by simply signing up on our website www.warmuptheworkplace.com.

Warming Up
The Workplace
by Frank and Susan Pastizzo

1

ATTITUDE

SNAPPING BEHAVIORS
Times When The Customer (and the rest of us) Can Be Wrong

"Kind words can be short and easy to speak, but their echoes are truly endless." —Mother Teresa

Picture the clerk, standing at the customer service desk, with her blue smock and name tag, complete with embroidered happy face and "Have a Nice Day!" slogan. She, like most, wants to be seen as a person and not just as the role she is playing. She wants to be recognized first for having human sensitivity and thought.

In his book I and Thou, Martin Buber discussed the beholding of a person as a "Thou," which is choosing to accept another as being worthy of the same regard we bestow upon our inner circle of friends and family members and ourselves. Buber also discussed seeing another person as an *It*. When we see people as *Its*, we disregard their human sensitivity and thought and view them merely as being means to some ends within the agendas that fill our days. Being on the receiving end of such disregard and indifference can be disheartening. Our clerk in her blue smock can attest to that. It has happened so often she has trouble maintaining her enthusiasm as new customers approach with money in their pockets, and the preconceived notion that "The Customer Is Always Right" embroidered on their very souls.

Each of us has, at some time, been left standing in line and ignored, as two clerks engaged in a collegial conversation about a topic external to providing service to us, and we often do not even attempt to veil our irritation. Yet many of us in our own workplaces relish our own chumming behaviors and similarly make our students, patients, clients, ringing phones, and customers wait. The need for a sense of belonging and having our true selves acknowledged and stroked, abides in us all. Not recognizing the importance of warm human regard is the first step toward tyranny, and it is amazing how many of us will reflexively adopt a tyrant's countenance and mentally clap our hands together and insist upon service immediately.

However, as providers of service, we also at times look upon our customers with irritation, and only see them as being associated with this distasteful task called work, which is going to take us away from a more meaningful and rewarding daydream, social moment with a colleague, or some other aspect of our workplace that we find more fulfilling and enjoyable. It is certain that many workers greet the prospect of helping a new customer or beginning a new service with a mental, or actual, heavy sigh and rolling of their eyes. Providing service is so painful for some, they become unconsciously (or purposefully) cruel and transmit their own irritation to their customers by embarking on power trips. They find ways to illuminate their customers' ignorance of their workplace's standard operating procedures. Examples of this can be found with sandwich makers who insist you follow their ordering procedures. (By no means should any of us let them know what type of cheese we want prior to informing them of our bread type, size of sandwich, and meat choices.) Not to do so will earn you the *sub shop snap*. Also, we should take care to never approach a forms clerk without ensuring we have really completed the form. Otherwise, we will be scolded for our intolerable incompleteness and made to perform the *motor vehicle maneuver*, where we have to return to the narrow wall counter to add one more word and number, and then rejoin the roped off line, like cattle at an auction, and shuffle back to the gates of clerkdom in hopes of bureaucratic redemption. Regrettably, these types of indifferent and snapping behaviors are often modeled during the orientation processes for new employees and become fused with the service.

Treating people with distaste, indifference, disregard, and disrespect can become the norm in many of our world's fast-paced interactions. The targeted recipients of these behaviors often feel snapped at, resulting in feelings of resentment, and the cycle then continues. It is up to us all, customer and service provider alike, to try to find ways to show people that they are not just *Its* to us, and learn to give acknowledgement with a smile and a quick, kind word. Finding the patience to allow people to be human and finish a brief conversation should not be such an affront. Asking a clerk what time his day started or pointing at a family picture and asking about his children only takes a second, and allowing time to listen and reply to his response is often all it takes to let a person know that you see him as a person and appreciate his help. Likewise, regarding our customers as valuable people, who will benefit from our help and kindness, will keep us feeling connected with the spirit of community. By taking a few seconds to reintroduce humanity into our brief encounters, we can reorient ourselves to appropriate conduct with one another, and recapture the essence of human service.

2

WHY?—
A Dangerous Idea?

"Whatever we hold precious, we cannot protect it from our curiosity, because being who we are, one of the things we deem precious is the truth. Our love of truth is surely a central element in the meaning we find in our lives."—Daniel Dennett, <u>Darwin's Dangerous Idea</u>

It is natural for us to seek answers and to know the why of things. In his book <u>Darwin's Dangerous Idea</u>, Dr. Daniel Dennett of Tuft's University explores reasons why we sometimes are resistant to new ideas, especially those that don't mesh with our existing ways of thinking. He also points out that as humans, we respect and honor the truth, and that things cannot be precious to us unless we can examine them.

In the workplace, when people are made to subscribe to or to do something without explanation, they are being asked to take a leap of faith, and to do what another says, based upon trust or recognition of authority. No one would deny that there are situations where *just do it* is a necessary concept, usually to save a life, save some money, save some time, or save face, and almost always, it should only be justified as an emergency measure when there isn't time to explain. But at some point, people will want to know the why of it all.

Under normal circumstances, people become apprehensive if they are not permitted to examine and think for themselves and stir things around on their own experiential palates a little. Not to give people an opportunity to do so causes them to feel resentment--that they are being perceived as not qualified to understand or that the concepts are somehow above them. We believe the case can be made that if a person seeks to understand, then he or she is entitled to an explanation, which will in turn satisfy the healthy curiosity that contributes to enthusiasm and buy-in. Regardless of their limitations, people will absorb as much as they can, building on what they already do understand, and feel respected as a result of the process.

Perhaps a case can also be made that there are times when leaders can justifiably conceal agendas and explanations to conserve scarce resources of time and energy, or to effectively deal with crisis situations. However, at some point, explanations need to be given to those who seek them-- explanations that stand the test of respectfulness and go beyond "because I said so."

There is no absolute right way or wrong way to deal with scarcity of time for offering explanations. Each of us has to try to read and respect others' timelines, deadlines, and current states of mental occupation. But as leaders, we have to make time, sometime, to let people know details of why we are doing certain things in certain ways, and allow people to satisfy their curiosity and to contribute their own ideas and recommendations. If this is done, all employees will tend to be more respectful of leadership, giving trust that they have best interests at heart, and accepting that there will be instances where they cannot afford the time or energy to explain why, show the fine print, and justify courses of action.

Explaining why is not a dangerous idea. Rather, it ensures that respect is the key element in this evolving process we call work.

Around Service Lines

"A hundred times every day I remind myself that my inner and outer life depend on the labors of other men and women, living and dead, and that I must exert myself in order to give in the measure as I have received and am still receiving."—Albert Einstein

Entering a hospital or a school can be somewhat intimidating if one is not used to it. These facilities are the places where the public comes in contact with the educated-- those who have been trained to observe objectively and to make judgments such as diagnoses of illnesses or levels of competency and learning. The hosts of these facilities have developed individual styles and manners for dealing with the public. Some are jovial. Some are neutral. Most are respectful and kind. The impression we make on the public and how we treat members of our own communities is very important. They enter into our domains of expertise, and we need to be patient and thorough listeners, respectful explainers of our processes, and kind conveyors of our professions.

Throughout our communities, all of us have been subjected to behaviors of people who are not happy with providing service. Some seem angry for having to be awake. There are some who flaunt their superiority of knowledge of their own processes and who treat those who are on the outside as, well, outsiders. Once, when I was presenting to a group of city managers and department heads, the Fire Chief and Chief of Police openly ridiculed the stupidity of people who would drive over a fire hose that was stretched across a street. Right away, I asked why. I did not know that the pressure of water through a fire hose was not strong enough to withstand a vehicle's weight. If there were no signs around and no one to instruct me, I probably would have driven over a fire hose and not realized it was a bad thing to do. They both looked at me, and one actually rolled his eyes. I was suddenly not welcome in their club. Being so on the ready to ridicule those ignorant of our own ways is arrogance on guard. Whether we are ordering a sandwich at a deli, filling out a motor-vehicle form, trying to pick a coffee style at Starbucks, negotiating through orange cones in a construction zone, applying for a loan, or attempting to find our way through a Health Proxy document... we do not always know the right thing to do, and we often look for someone to give some guidance. How that guidance is given is paramount and displays the level of respect, leadership, and unity of an organization.

All of us are tasked with being community representatives. Our manners of engagement with one another are either representative of accessibility and respectful concern or of some type of restrictive aloofness and specialized arrogance. It's worth examining the manners around each of our lines of service.

"The Help"

"Human beings, by changing the inner attitudes of their minds, can change the outer aspects of their lives."—William James

When I hear about LL Bean customer service, I often wonder how someone is trained to be absolutely unflappable in the face of neutral, unappreciative, or even hostile behaviors from unaffected and irate customers. One thing is for sure: many companies have learned the long-term value of providing superior customer service and how it builds and grows a loyal customer base. These companies have empowered their employees with the abilities to make their transactions favor those they serve, almost without exception. This in turn keeps people coming back and their reputation grows through word of mouth.

What about the constancy at which employees like this behave? I've encountered this constancy with professionals in all fields: this willingness to dedicate one's self to the service of another and to not be distracted from this dedication by anything. People like this are present throughout our communities. They're in nursing homes, hospitals, cafeterias, fire and police departments, stores, factories, schools, banks, churches, volunteer groups, hotels, etc. There is an attitude of acceptance and sincerity in service exuded that actually trumps the prickly, ugly, snappy, or snobbish attitudes which arise with people from time to time. I've often thought a good working definition of a professional is someone who performs at a constant despite distractions.

I was recently inspired by a group of professionals who lead auxiliary workers in a university setting. I imagine the egos walking through that environment and the difficulty of being the food service worker on the service line in a university where some of the students and faculty do not see you at all. To them, you're "the help," and they are only passing through on their way to a better future or to more important matters. If it were me in that 2080-hour annual role, I would have to try my best to *LL Bean it* and try to absolutely shine and make connections and build relationships and design my environment to be one where I and others enjoy being. My smile and welcomes and fun would be my lapel buttons, proudly saying, "Yes. I'm the help. How can I help you?" I would set a kind tone to try to model some behavioral expectations. Rudeness would become irrelevant on my service line.

It is a worry that some employees choose alternative mind-sets, reside in resentment, stay on the defensive, and make subtle or open retaliations, hence contributing to a negative and backward momentum and continuing to perpetuate employment turnover.

I believe all of us have our own service lines, and in the face of our service provision we will encounter many different attitudes. By dedicating ourselves professionally, each of us can find a constant at which to perform that designs an environment—a work and life environment—that's to our own liking. We get what we give.

5

AVOIDING THE SNAP TRAP

"You do not lead by hitting people over the head—that's assault, not leadership."—Dwight D. Eisenhower

I n the midst of busy workplaces, people sometimes get highly passionate and feel a need to stress the importance of their own processes. Often, in this stressing, some can become dismissive and disrespectfully snappy to people who are participating in their processes. Having been recipients of such dressing-down behaviors, we think it would be a good staff development and empathy-building exercise to have people experience some of the snapping behaviors one finds in certain airport security processes, medical facilities, deli lines, and bureaucratic screening procedures. It could be useful to have people experience how it feels to be at their most vulnerable moment of confusion, and receive some facial expression or statement that implies they must be complete idiots for not understanding what was just explained to them over the last eight seconds.

In the fall of 2002, we were entering a conference center in Manhattan to deliver a presentation on the upper floors and had equipment to bring up from our van. Not knowing how to gain access, I approached a woman at the front security desk, who was sitting behind thick security glass. She impatiently gestured for me to pick up an exterior telephone handset to speak to her. Upon placing the phone to my ear, her first shouted words were: "You're tying up the phone, sir!"

As we become seasoned in our careers and become more and more familiar with our own ways of doing things, we may become less and less patient with those who are not up to speed. We seem less inclined to invest face-to-face time in explaining things. We create orientation and procedural manuals intensified with barking words like, "you must" and "under no circumstances should you ever," Ironically, many of the manuals we take so much time to produce, quickly become obsolete due to new developments in our constantly changing lives.

Being an authority in some arena or subject matter does not release us from our responsibility to be respectful. Saying things like, "I know this process seems a bit automated and cold. It's just to keep things running smoothly and save time. I'll help you through this if you get stuck...don't worry," justifies our authority and lets people know that we still respect them and that we are still connected to humanity. We need to avoid seeing our processes as ends in themselves, rather than being means to achieving efficient and effective outcomes.

Take a look at your own processes. Are your new employees oriented by patient, respectful mentors or by snappy know-it-alls who model eye-rolling arrogance and intolerance for rookies? Taking good care of people needs to be on the top of our to-do lists.

It's easy to get rushed and fall into the Snap Trap. It takes only a moment to say a few words to make it okay again. Toning down our urgency is more often appropriate than not. Certainly we can all find areas where we can lighten up and warm it up a little more. There will still be plenty for us to be passionate about.

6

Showing What You Want To See

"There is so much good in the worst of us, and so much bad in the best of us, that it hardly behooves any of us to talk about the rest of us."—*Edward Wallis Hoch*

The next time you find yourself getting ready to unload or vent your frustration, anger, or resentment to someone or a group of people in your workplace, see if you can find the presence of mind to ask yourself, "Do I have the right to taint this environment and the attitudes of the people I am around with my negative spin?"

It is very human to express frustration and anger when things don't go the way we hope—just watch Tiger Woods when he miss-hits one of his drives. One of my friends has a good rule on the golf course. He calls it the thirty-second rule. When the bad shot inevitably comes, the player is entitled thirty seconds to rant, but no more than that. Then he or she needs to be respectful of others so that the bad attitude does not bleed into the rest of the group. I usually find eight seconds to be more than enough time for me to yell or just plain laugh at myself. I usually get a few minutes worth every round.

Most of us find it helpful to have someone we can powwow with to get things off of our chests. Many of us can help each other by allowing others to use us as their sounding boards once in a while. We can offer some encouragement, and help them and ourselves to move on. But we all have the professional responsibility to keep the peace and promote a flowing work environment by modeling the attitudes we want to see in others.

Things will not always go as we hope, and we may need to take half a minute to show our disappointment. Then we need to find our new directions and go forward from there.

Avoid the negative conversations in break rooms, hallways, and parking lots. Find ways to generate and stay in a positive flow through your days. You'll find you can create a positive space around yourself and pass that energy on to others. If you find yourself frequently carrying negative ideas and thoughts and ready to pass them off to others, ask yourself why you feel the need to perpetuate that kind of negative energy.

We get what we give. We see what we show. Pass around the good stuff.

7

Calm in the Center

"Men acquire a particular quality by constantly acting a particular way
... you become just by performing just actions, temperate by performing
temperate actions, brave by performing brave actions." —Aristotle

Are you a busy person with a full agenda fraught with numerous distractions that interfere with your focus during crucial decision-making times? Do these distractions sometimes make you lash out, slam doors, make mistakes, bark, or be less than cordial with your fellow workers or customers?

When our grandson was three-months-old he had cranial surgery and was admitted to a pediatric intensive care unit for twenty-four hours, where a team of splendid human beings juggled their agendas, his care, and our hearts in a stunning routine that should be displayed in high-definition TV. It was every bit as spectacular as Cirque du Soleil, with many more real risks. There was no lashing, slamming, or barking...

Here's an analogy: You are driving on an icy road with a tailgater behind you. You come around a corner and see a tractor-trailer jackknifed, a car in the ditch, a herd of deer standing in the road, and a two-year old toddling about on the center line, looking for her mommy. In your car, you have frantic family members screaming directions about what you should do next. You reassure your passengers, touch your brakes gently a couple of times, guide your car to the left lane and shoulder, stop, get out, gather up the two-year old with a calming hug and return her to her mom, shoo the deer away to safety, and console the angry tailgater who ran into the guard rail and totaled his car. You continue to care for anyone else needing your help, and then drive your car and your family further on your journey.

Our tiny little grandson was smiling and discharged from the hospital the next day and sent home to wear a special helmet throughout the next year. Our awesome team of workers at the University Health System in San Antonio continues in their special journey, driving many other families through perilous circumstances. We thank them with all of our hearts for their dedication, professionalism, and incredible bedside manner.

People have the ability to learn and develop personal tools that keep them in control under the most frantic of circumstances. They can maintain their cool *and* their warmth. They have presence of mind and heart. When these talented and experienced people are present, the calm is contagious, and we leave them hopeful that some of their gifts will remain with us.

8

"BECAUSE I SAID SO"
How Bossiness Kicks People Off The Team

*"Rank does not confer privilege or give power. It imposes responsibility."—
Peter F. Drucker*

Once I joined a group of nineteen friends for a three-day golf vacation in Northern California. Comprising largely high school and community college teachers, some interesting group dynamics surfaced and fluctuated during our stay. Most of the time it was the bliss of a group of friends enjoying play. At other times, when some impromptu organizing was needed, a few would employ a-- *my way or the highway style*--, and the playful mood would be kicked away. Some would respond by actually walking away from the group with the classic hangdog look of a dejected teenager. In one instance, having the luxury of being new to the group and thus not feeling a need to comply with some established, on-vacation authority, I asked, "Jeez, when did my old cub scout pack leader get here?" This brought a chuckle from some and defensive anger from the man. "Frank, you used to teach, right? You know you need to yell at kids sometimes to get them to pay attention!" I did not respond. Some of the "kids" walking away seemed response enough.

A good friend who is a school principal once made this observation about teachers: their clientele never gets older, while they themselves inevitably do. This means that each year the same adolescent behaviors surface from their customers, and while during their initial years as educators they may have found some delight in the raw, youthful energy of kids, after a few years, for some, their patience dwindles. Present in this environment for their entire careers, they develop reflexive snapping behaviors to quell disruption or confusion. Accustomed to being the only one speaking and in control of a group, they assert this stance, even amongst their peers, at the drop of a hat. We need to consider how often and how much this type of snapping behavior is routinely modeled, absorbed, and employed by all of us, perhaps as a result of being immersed in similar environments during our formative years.

What is encouraging is the demonstrated ability of people to hear themselves and say things like, "Sorry, that came out a little harsh..." We all need to take care to hear ourselves and be aware of how we respond to disruption and confusion. When we react with harshness, one may reflexively get in step and follow our barked command and another may simply walk away. Both will most likely feel kicked.

9

THE ATTITUDE
IS THE MESSAGE

"Language exerts hidden power, like a moon on the tides."—Rita Mae Brown

Once during a presentation for an association of county and municipal employees, I demonstrated what I intended to be a kind and respectful manner, as I did some supervisory role-playing. The point of the exercise was to show how leaders could impart equality as they give direction. When the seminar attendee and I had finished our scene, I asked the other attendees for an evaluation of my manner as I had played the role. One responded, "Not bad." Another responded, "Demeaning." The disparity between these two interpretations clearly demonstrated the human tendency to project one's own past experiences into the present. To one attendee, my manner during the role-play activity reflected equality and respect and was acceptable based on her frame of reference. To the other person, something in my demeanor caused her to recognize some trait or nuance that she interpreted as being belittling or condescending.

We have noticed that when someone is asked, "What did he or she say?" that the response often first relates the attitude that was communicated. "She was very understanding." "He was pretty demanding." "She seemed too busy to care about my problem." The specific details of conversations come second. First, we often hear the report of the perceived attitude that significantly colored the meaning of the actual words. If a person perceives a discrepancy between the two, it is the attitude that trumps.

We all quite naturally read between the lines in our encounters, picking up on subtle clues beyond the direct message. It is one of the skills we develop as we gain experience. All of us need to be aware that another person can get a completely inaccurate impression of our meaning, due to perceived yet unintended attitudes coming from us. Do we sometimes inject a little sarcasm into a moment that calls for complete sincerity? Do we break eye contact and look at our watches or our day's to-do list when people need us to be locked on to their concerns? Do we at times come across as being demeaning?

Sometimes we are in a rush. We think someone should be able to find what seems to be an obvious solution to a problem. Maybe at these times, when we are likely not to be in our best forms, we should postpone the pending interaction and allow a moment to polish ourselves and try our best to project sincerity and kindness. When positive attitudes become prevalent, they will be an important part of every message.

Abruptness Forgiven

"Laughter is the closest distance between two people." —*Victor Borge*

One early Sunday afternoon in February, six or seven years ago, at about -18 degrees, a block from the St. Lawrence River, at the top of New York State, Susan and I were dabbling in the kitchen, making some fresh guacamole. We had smushed and chopped the elephant garlic and cilantro, squeezed a lime and blended in the avocado, sampled some, corrected the seasonings, and sampled more. It dawned on me that in spite of our Sunday tradition, none of our family had called to check in. So I stepped into the dining room to make a few calls. The phone was dead. I went to the living room to try our cordless, and it worked fine, so thinking the dining room phone must have just been off the hook, I returned to it, only to find it was still not working.

Now my agenda shifted to having the phone fixed. I returned to the cordless phone and dialed the phone company, whose name I will not mention, but it rhymes with horizon. The dispatcher informed me that it would be sometime during the day on Monday when a repair person would be sent. Not even seven minutes after I had hung up, there was a knock at our door, and there stood a telephone repairman, who apparently had been in town, and had pulled in our driveway to check out our problem.

He had the thickest and loudest New York City accent I had ever heard. "What's the problem with your phone, Sir?" I handed him the phone, and he listened to the dead air. "Oh, your phone's not wookin'? I then handed him the cordless. He listened. "But your cordless is wookin'? That's biz-ahh, sir. That's biz-ahh."

"I'm going to pool the truck up to the house, Sir. If I can fix the problem from outside, there will be no chahge. If the problem is with the equipment, you'll have to fix that yourself. Is that acceptable to you Sir?" I agreed. I couldn't resist asking him where he was from. He replied, "Oh, you like my southern accent? I'm from the south Bronx!" He went outside to bring his truck closer to our house, and Susan and I immediately decided that we liked this curt but attentive character, who had chosen to help us at the drop of a hat in such extremely frigid temperatures.

He was back at our door ten minutes later. "Sir, get your coat on, I wanna show you somethin'." Susan and I shared a smile, and out into the driveway I went with him. The wind was coming off the river and the wind chill was around thirty below. I partially blocked the wind from him while he showed me his voltage meter as he connected it to various wires.

"Sir, do you understand circuits?"

"Yes I do."

"Well each of these wires makes a circuit. These two wires are your cordless phone. Do you see this meter?

"Yup."

"That's a short circuit. Your cordless phone is shorting out your other phone line. Do you understand what a short circuit is?"

"Yes I do."

He turned and faced me. Sir, you're my customer. I mean no disrespect ..., but you need a breath mint."

I had not seen that coming. It caught me by total surprise. I started to laugh as I realized the guacamole had kicked in and he was directly down wind from me. As I laughed harder in appreciation for his honesty and apologized for my garlic breath, he felt he had to explain himself more.

"Again sir, I mean no disrespect, you're my customer, but the wind is coming off the river there and it's blowin' right in my face." Now I was totally laughing and assured him that I was not offended and that I found his honesty, along with his excellent customer service, wonderful.

In retrospect, years later, I still think back to how this man was able to first treat us as being special by finding a way into our hearts, and then, be completely abrupt and, because of the connection we felt, not seem offensive at all. There is a certain quality of familiarity that, if cultivated respectfully between people, can allow an awful lot to be forgiven. It always seems to start with one part honest service being coupled with one part authenticity and another part humor. When those ingredients are combined, you'll have a great human recipe.

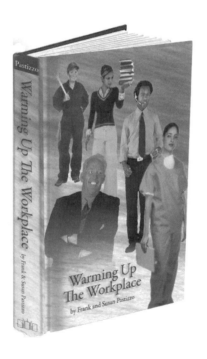

Warming Up
The Workplace

by Frank & Susan Pastizzo

2

GROUP
CONSCIOUSNESS

1

Going to Work

I'm going to work today.
I need to bring my brightest and my best.

"Man is so made that he can only find relaxation from one kind of labor by taking up another."—Anatole France

Stresses in our home lives can muddle our abilities to do the above. There are worries about children and grandchildren and bills and college and home maintenance and family health concerns and pet ailments and births and funerals and school issues and problems with the car...

All of us seek stability in these areas, and everyone coming through the door at work is dealing with these same issues. Some have friends at work who are good listeners and who take some time to help them with their difficulties so they can re-stabilize. Some use good, hard work as their escape. Some find ways to revitalize themselves through intense concentration and study. Some plunge into physical activity.

Whether it's a school, factory, office, health center, or farm, when people get together to do work, we quickly find ways to minimize our personal screens and work on the professional tasks at hand. It increases the structure in our lives. It results in community production and community accomplishments. It can temporarily take us out of our own complications or instabilities, refocus the strongest parts of us, and give us valuable time and perspective from a group-energized place of order. Ideally, we incorporate our group's positive momentums into our personal circles. We come up with new plans and resolutions and bring more considerate, decisive, and positive energies back to our home lives.

Understanding that work can have this revitalizing effect, it is hugely important that we each strive to create and protect our workplaces so that they contain and preserve these kinds of rejuvenating energies. We all need to remain respectful of this group space and its far-reaching functions and its place in the community continuum. If we cannot create in our work culture an environment where each of us can do our work at our best, then we should be perhaps looking harder to find somewhere where we can.

Going to work and communing with others requires all of us to honor the environment and to be at our brightest and our best. When we do it well, we bring home the same for ourselves and send home the same with others. Thus, going to work is an incredibly important part of an energizing cycle in life. It's where many perform at their most constant, which helps all of us.

2

LOOKING FOR BETTER WAYS
The Perpetual Search for High Standards

"We must use time as a tool, not as a crutch."—John F. Kennedy

"Y ou've outdone yourself!" When an individual or a team hears these three words, and the person saying them really means them, the joy stemming from the recognition is unmistakable. Those being recognized experience feelings of worth and completion, along with a good sense of purpose and confidence for the future. Chances are, this outdoing of self was attributed to a work environment where people are supportive of each other's attempts at innovation. Later, during a moment with a friend, there will probably be an exchange that might sound something like this: "You will not believe what we came up with today…!"

I would like to outdo myself each day and have outdoing myself as my daily goal. It would be splendid to stretch and tap into some synergistic life force that seems outside of myself and feel a sense of freedom to explore ways that are new to me and make tiny, daily improvements in the ways I do everything. I would hope associates would not view me as being a maverick or think I was seeing myself as somehow better than the status quo or above the existing rules. After all, I am not seeking credit; but rather, I am trying to discover and incorporate new energies outside of myself. I am immersing myself in the here and now and trying to learn and be part of the good energy around me.

When people feel such a sense of freedom, performance levels soar. When people are given regular invitations to think of better ways to do things, they feel valued and often begin using more regions of their brains. They become much more mindful of what's going on around them. They listen to other people's ideas and begin to see new possibilities. With time and freedom, many people are able to come up with all sorts of innovations.

"We Don't Have Time For This"

Imagine a new person on an assembly line who has precisely eighty-five seconds to complete the assembling of an air conditioner cowl. On his third morning of work at his new job, as the seventieth unit approaches, young Mr. Ganther gets an idea that if the unit was to come to his and the next three stations in a different position of angle, thirty seconds or more could be shaved off the production time at his station alone. During his break, he approaches the line manager with the idea. The idea is summarily dismissed. A condescending smile is delivered to the new guy. A brief reason is given. "It would cost too much to re-machine the line to flip the conditioners, and we don't have time for it."

Eventually, the idea grew and was submitted via another route. Within a year, a Ganther Flipper was installed at three separate positions, saving over one hundred and seven minutes of handling time each day at eleven stations, allowing an additional one hundred and sixteen units to be manufactured per day. Upon further evaluation one year later, fewer injuries were reported due to the elimination of the previous lifting and turning that each worker performed.

How many good ideas are never brought forward because people are afraid of shabby treatment if they break rank? How many timesaving ideas are thrown away immediately because we don't have time to listen? Finding ways to instill time in each work week for people at all levels to formulate ideas and then come together and discuss strategies will have several benefits. Among these are:

> Teambuilding and appreciation of talent at all levels.
>
> New people + New eyes on existing ways =
> New and perhaps better ways
>
> People at all levels feeling included and valued

Standards of Operation and Human Error

No matter how rigid standards of operation are, sometimes horrible, human errors will happen. To respond to such errors with blame and more rigidity is natural; but often, by using team collaboration and brainstorming, safeguards and better systems are created by the same people involved in the initial mistakes. While we do need people to instill operating standards and teach others the basics and promote understanding of procedures, we also need these same people to be ever mindful of their our own fallibilities during these processes. We can easily get caught up in the intoxication of momentum and go off in totally wrong directions. We must be continually open to the spontaneous questions and occurrences and involvement from all levels, which can ignite both creativity and caution. We can find ways to eliminate the negative connotations of team scrutiny contained in phrases like stepping on someone's toes, invading one's turf, or looking over somebody's shoulder, etc. Having other people available to collaborate with and to check our work to reduce errors, promote safety, and improve final outcomes needs to be a welcomed constant. Fearing scrutiny and hiding mistakes is self-destructive to both the individual and the organization. Allowing for others to be aware of our individual strengths and weaknesses helps us to cover for each other and become a stronger team. The environment is then safe for true collaboration.

Is it okay for an operating room technician to ask an ophthalmologist if she is certain she is about to operate on the correct eye? Perhaps thirty (or even five) years ago it would have been taboo for an orderly to question a doctor; however status barriers like this are quickly becoming obsolete. Now, more and more, all people of an organization are asked to speak freely and give regular input. From many ideas come good ideas. In hospitals, on this very day, possibly more than five people will assure that they are operating on the correct limb, using the proper blood type, and have the right patient. The team gets together and shares as much information as possible from all aspects of care and makes good, synergistic decisions.

In life we will always find ourselves having to make immediate decisions that will dramatically impact other people. Each situation often has some unique slant to it that will call for spontaneous tailoring to make it right and good for the people involved. Procedure manuals are rarely referred to in this dynamic of life. Rather, we strive to remember what's important and to be effective in the here and now. People are obligated to speak up and stretch themselves into action in the space surrounding us all. And at the end of the day, we will all feel the accomplishment of being such an important part of that space and celebrate the outdoing of ourselves.

3

Joy in Solitude

"Treat people the way they want to be treated, not the way you would want to be treated."—Anne Bruce

Anne Bruce's direction is certainly challenging when you run into a person with an opposing agenda to your own. There are times when it is very hard to follow one's own advice.

I was on the golf course once with another man who works for a large corporation and who had no idea that my career was dedicated to helping people find ways to make their workplaces reflect the joy and values of their life places. This friend of mine was venting about certain *types* of people in his plant he classified as *cheerleaders* in a *popularity contest* who spent large portions of their careers prompting laughter and insisting upon spontaneous bubbly-eyed glee. These people, he went on, were demanding of attention from everyone, and constantly prodded each person to *match* their own manic exuberance.

I really listened with all my heart for the next couple of holes. I never argued, but prompted him to tell me more. He did, and I learned so much. He demonstrated his exasperation with these *types*, by saying, "C'mon already, I'm **at work here!**" He went on to say he did not enjoy going to office parties or meeting with people for drinks after work. Regarding some of these people in the office who corner him with their urgent invitations to participate in gatherings, he said "The truth is, I might not *like* them and I don't feel like socializing with them much while we're at work and certainly not at *all* during my private time."

Finally, in his scathing indictment of workplace society, he said he should have the right to come to work and *work*. He should feel okay about focusing and concentrating on his job, reserving his socializing and playing with those few he chooses. And if the *cheerleaders* think he is a *non-team player*, is *uncooperative*, or has an *attitude problem*, they're wrong. And if they report to others that he is any of the above, then *they are the ones with the attitude problem*. Their labeling his non-participation as problematic is *the problem*. Don't they have jobs to do?

I found myself re-examining some of my own frequent attempts at play while at work. I thought of other friends of mine who even exceeded my own antics. And I thought of some other people who might have been expensively interrupted as a result. As we explore ways to bring joy into the workplace, we still need to promote choice and allow people to maintain their own styles. We all have a responsibility to be polite and sociable to those with whom we spend a significant portion of time each day. For most of us, this includes family and workmates. We all need to focus on adding to, rather than detracting from, a positive environment. Sometimes we can add the most by respecting people's privacy.

Anne Bruce's quote has far-reaching applications, and we should strive to appreciate individual styles and minimize the forcing of our own agendas no matter how seemingly innocent they may be. When people are at work, they are captive audiences. They have limited choices in what they hear, see, or participate in. To attempt to force another to show false enthusiasm can be insulting. To insist upon the extraction of glee from another can be disrespectful. Some people in workplaces may not like one another. There are some who enjoy a simple, quiet conversation over lunch with a single co-worker and then function best when returning to their work in peace and quiet. Most people tend to group toward the middle of the two extremes of solitude and gregariousness; however, those on the far ends deserve respect, too.

Respecting one another is the key. We continually have opportunities to display our own preferences in positive ways to help our co-workers better understand who we are. People who appreciate, allow, and accommodate other styles are at the center of functional teams.

4

TALKING POINTS

"If you want to build a ship, don't drum up the men to gather wood, divide the work, and give orders. Instead, teach them to yearn for the vast and endless sea."—Antoine de Saint-Exupéry

Frank and I frequently spend the first hour of our workday seemingly relaxing in our chairs, doing no visible work, just discussing issues that are on our minds relative to current events and the world situation. Because we have our own business, our work and our lives are melded into one, and how we delegate our time for work tasks is totally up to us. We are realizing that the more significantly interested and active in world affairs we become, the more we contemplate our own day-to-day activities. While our discussions frequently center on current events and not on details of our jobs, we always come around to the question of what our driving purpose is, and how our daily work relates to the issues of our time. It often seems a stretch to relate some perceived good that our work accomplishes to any significant contribution to the big picture; however, we do hold that all services are human services, and each of us doing our small part for the betterment of humanity does have a considerable effect. It is this conviction that keeps us motivated to behave as though we are in life, and not just in a workplace.

Since our lifestyle allows us time to have discussions while we are at work, we have become aware that most people do not have this option once they have entered their workplaces for the day. There are too many tasks to get done to justify spending time conversing about the all-important but seemingly irrelevant world scene. We believe that through heartfelt conversations, understanding how one's individual job contributes to making the world a better place, also helps employees see how their jobs contribute to their entire organization—be it a nursing home, a school, a bank, or a restaurant. If employees are motivated to think beyond their job tasks to how they connect with their community and the world around them, the increase of consciousness results in creativity and problem-solving which more than justifies the time spent in the conversations.

How do leaders help employees understand their importance to the success of the organization? If employees were to spend a part of each workday involved in talking points relevant to their lives, workplaces, and communities, with no required outcome beyond discussion, they would be more likely to become ship builders (world connectors), rather than just wood-gatherers. The positive spin-off would be productive beyond measure.

5

Is It Written in Stone?

"Change is not merely necessary to life, it is life." —*Alvin Toffler*

How many times in our workplaces are our reasons for doing certain things in certain ways based on the fact that it's our policy, it's in our mission statement, it's in the contract, or it's always the way it's been done...? When policies are written and agreed upon by a designated group, they often hold an aura of permanence, and take on a protective barrier, which seems to say, "Look, a lot of experienced and important people worked really hard on these rules for a long time, so do not dare to question, change, or bend them in the least."

In the Foreword to Jon Stewart and *The Daily Show's* America, (The Book), none other than our beloved Thomas Jefferson has risen from his 182-year-old grave to address the "myth of infallibility" we tend to embrace when we think of the founders of our institutions. About the writing of the Constitution, the author expounds, "Do you know why we called them amendments? Because they amend! They fix mistakes or correct omissions and they themselves can be changed. If we had meant for the Constitution to be written in stone we would have written it in stone."

He further advises not to coast on the accomplishments of our predecessors, but instead, to work as hard as they did to keep what they created evolving and relevant. There it is again, this need to keep our decisions and policies evolving and relevant. Remember what Mark Twain said about it not making much sense to chart a course when you're on a river? How many times have each of us been at meetings when someone presents his or her latest volume of work representing many hours of surveying work systems, researching past strategies, etc., and we praise their huge efforts and accept their work and proposals for new ways of doing things? And then, a week or month or even a year later, someone notices a flaw in the new system and tries to point out that the new policy needs to be changed but is quickly hushed due to the amount of time someone spent to put the current policy in place. Sometimes, people work long and hard on ideas that are wrong. Sometimes, good ideas become irrelevant in a short time. How long do we think it will take before the Federal Aviation Administration modifies its regulations so passengers can be given the benefit of the doubt that they know how to fasten seatbelts without a demonstration? We also have not been permitted to smoke on planes now for over ten years. How long will they continue to remind us? Now there is no doubt that the Federal Aviation Administration is important and works hard, but it is not infallible and some of its practices need to be renewed and updated from time to time. Some get very defensive and annoyed when their policies are ridiculed. But no more annoyed than those being subjected to them. By continuing with outdated policies, we can cause much more than annoyance.

It is interesting to us that people in a meeting will get focused on a point such as work schedules and go on and on and around and around, and finally someone will make a decision and it will be agreed upon by most (after all, we've been in here for hours), and the group goes on to the final checklist at the tail end of the meeting. However, one team member has been contemplating the previous decision, and during the final moments, she says, "I'm sorry, but I need to go back to the scheduling issue." There is a collective groan, some statement is made about beating a dead horse, and then she points out the significant flaw in the decision that will have a ripple effect and cause a huge overtime issue on the second shift in four facilities. Often, instead of being grateful to the person for thinking more and saving us from a potential catastrophe, there is sarcastic chiding from some for making the meeting go longer. Maybe the person is asked to research the problem in more depth on her own and come up with some recommendations (this shows everyone the extra work that is assigned when one thinks on her own and over-participates.)

Perhaps we need to go to the blackboard more often and write our policies in *chalk* and then walk through our days with erasers handy to keep our instituted policies current with the days and lives of those affected by them. The next time something seems to be going against the grain at work, take the time to examine the reasons, and if it's just because someone says it's written in stone or that's always the way we've done it around here, maybe it's time to do some amending.

6

MEETING EXPECTATIONS

"When people talk, listen completely. Most people never listen." —Ernest Hemingway

W hen we ask our audiences, "What is the first thing on your mind when you sit down for a meeting?" many members respond, "When will we get out of here?" or simply, "How long is this going to last?" It seems to be common human nature. Many do not like the prospect of giving up their individual time to sit down for a work-related meeting. Some, in a rush to finish, become the most agreeable beings on the planet, perpetually avoiding conflict, in order to shoot through the agenda. One person told us once that his idea of a successful meeting was to leave with no new tasks assigned.

All of us are busy people. We have incredibly complex, personal and professional to-do lists, and it's no wonder we dread the prospect of taking time out of our days to be reminded that there is still more to be done. We also, in our growing familiarity with our many different colleagues, become contemptuous of those certain behaviors that rub us the wrong way, further deterring us from wanting to come together.

Just as we sometimes forget to see a person as a person, rather than an agenda item, we tend to look at a meeting as a collection of agenda items, and not as an entity of its own. Good meetings are synergistic—what comes out of them should be greater than the sum of the individual ideas of the participants. When we simply tick off item after item until we get to the bottom of the list, the synergy doesn't happen. Often we look at a meeting as just another task to do, rather than an opportunity to use the resources of many minds to work on our collective to-do lists.

The next time you find yourself dreading a meeting for whatever reason, we hope you will find these few ideas and attitude tips helpful:

● We redefine ourselves by how we act next. Bringing a bright and personable manner to the table can promote that same manner throughout the meeting.

● Do not come to a meeting with your mind made up. Mark Twain said it doesn't make sense to set a course when you're on a river. Come to listen, process new information, and respond with your own. It is a meeting, not a lecture hall.

● Work is part of life and it never ends. We will always be finding more that needs to be done. Don't feel overwhelmed. Even when we are multi-tasking, we can only address one task at a time.

● Remember that each person at the table has an incredibly complex, personal and professional agenda. Be respectful, kind, and appreciative that each has sat down to attempt to proceed together. Find ways you can contribute to make it a good meeting.

There will always be meetings. We all have the professional responsibility to make them functional and worthwhile, and to expect to come out of them with more than we brought in. Sometimes we gain some additional tasks; however, if it was a good meeting, we have helped each other, solved some problems, acquired some new ideas, and renewed our energy.

7

'ROUND TABLES

The quarterly meeting is called to order. The minutes from the last meeting are read. Then it is announced that each person is to report on his or her department's activities for the last quarter, what the department's current priorities are, and to briefly discuss a few short-term and longer-term goals.

The first report begins. You'll be the third person to give your report. You were ready for this. You have your notes in front of you. Your key points are well organized and you have some glowing numbers. You're a bit concerned about the reaction you'll get on your overtime usage during early November, but you probably won't be too far out of line with other departments, given the way the flu hit this year. Heck, your own kids were down for a week and out of school. Luckily, all of you are healthier now and will hopefully stay that way for your February family ski trip. (Someone enters the meeting late.) You think about how she is always late. There's no way she's going to be ready to give her report. She's too harried...

The previous scenario seems common enough for our beginning of the year meetings. Each of us around the table wants to be as prepared as possible to report on our progress and share our information with our team. The huge problem with this previous scenario though, is that our point of view character has not listened to his teammate's first report at all. To quote a former co-teacher, "We have virtual playgrounds going on in our minds." We really do need to try harder to come to our face to face meetings prepared to listen, especially when we consider how all of our work is inter-connected and how we may need to step up and assist our fellow team members in their department's priorities, should they be stricken with some life emergency.

For these reasons, here are a couple of meeting dos:

- **Come prepared to listen.**
- As much as possible, schedule meetings well in advance so people know the proposed agendas and can prepare. Avoid calling spontaneous meetings that require impromptu presentations. No one will be able to listen effectively. They'll be too busy mentally preparing their own reports.
- **Come prepared to listen.**
- If an emergency meeting must be called, limit the agenda to the emergency. Then, agree that any "quick draw" resolutions will be *interim* ones, and schedule another meeting after some time to really discuss the new resolution's merits and flaws. Then your group has had enough time to effectively put together an agency policy to handle whatever the new development was.
- **Come prepared to listen.**

We live in fast times with a myriad of interruptions. Let's not squander our opportunities when we have the luxury of meeting face-to-face. When we practice giving each other a level of regard where we actually imagine ourselves in the other's place, and we take notes and ask questions and respond with comments that show others that we are locked on to *their* stories, and not lost in our own playgrounds, we become truly informed and much better equipped to really work together.

8

'ROUND TABLES
PART II
People Trump Protocol

So the department reports have been given, and some general discussion of issues ensues. There are different ideas about what kind of meeting dynamic is the best. Some prefer sticking to agendas and agreed upon time constraints, going through items in a systematic manner, and minimizing discussion, recognizing that time is one of our most valuable commodities. Objectives are met, plans are implemented, and the immediate progress is documented.

Another type of meeting looks much more informal, where groups of people feel free to explore ideas, interject their own, and maybe even mix in a little personal conversation. They recognize there is a target time frame, but they do not let it interfere with the flow of ideas and the team building dynamic . It has a relaxed feel, but is still serious and on point. There is a level of trust whereby people feel free to think out loud, while still recognizing the right of all to take part.

The format of the first approach may seem the most efficient. The second format, however, has the potential for yielding much more inclusive and comprehensive results, because it allows people to interact and spin off each other. The concepts of scaffolding and synergy -- that a group is more than the sum of its members-- lead

60

many to experiment with loosening their meeting dynamics, having faith that people will come up with better and better ideas resulting from all freely contributing.

We always should be looking to help people bring out their best during meetings. Promoting the correct style of meeting for the type of work to be done is an important managerial skill. Adjustments to the tone around our tables can help people feel at ease and greatly enhance our valuable face-to-face time and productivity.

9

REAL EFFICIENCY
TAKES TIME

At a scheduled department head meeting once, seventeen of us sat around our table, rushing through our agenda, focused on getting through all of the business at hand, before departing to carry on in our more autonomous domains. A point of the meeting arrived unannounced, when we were asked to come up with a new company name for a subsidiary of our organization. This new name had to be marketable, while also conveying the mission of our company. Suddenly, the emotional climate around the table became more frantic as people tried to muse and started to shout out first blush ideas, while simultaneously adhering to a meeting schedule. It felt like a flashcard scenario from elementary school. This hurry-up so we can move on dynamic was a huge impediment to the flow-state, and although there was faith that a great name could be created, the feeling that we were racing was terribly confining and counter-productive. Sometimes deadlines live up to their name.

Returning to the theme of a previous chapter, the way meetings are conducted should vary in accordance with the work that needs to be accomplished. Sometimes we need to feel that we have time to explore. There is a target time frame, but it should not always dictate the flow of the meeting, and at times, needs to allow for a feeling of trust where people can think out loud. This dynamic can yield better results for certain group objectives, because it allows people to spin off of each other. Inevitably, someone will come up with a great thought based on the ideas, often seemingly unrelated, of people around him or her. A person may have a germinal concept that can take root because someone else has the knowledge or skills to fill in integral missing pieces.

Imagine the ideas that could flow if a company invited its entire workforce to have open discussions on the topics of customer service, operating efficiencies, schedules and staffing, supplies, storage, transportation, equipment sharing, etc. Might there be discoveries of better ways? Many try to avoid what seems to be the utter chaos that takes place during brainstorming. Some people are very guarded with their ideas and withhold them for a calculated time in order to bring more personal credit and recognition to themselves. Some people say there just isn't time enough to give everyone a say. Surely, in careers that span decades, there is time for all to contribute and join in the current of energy that flows through an organization, and to share in the rewards. Most often, company leaders only call their entire staff together to present previously made decisions, without giving an opportunity for everyone to chime in with what could be brilliant innovations. The best way to have a great idea is to have a lot of ideas.

Organizations need to stay current in times of perpetual change, and change occurs because of people and ideas. Opening channels and allowing people's ideas to flow with the current keeps us flexible and promotes real, rather than perceived efficiency.

10

PROFESSIONAL EXPECTATIONS

The great boxing coach Angelo Dundee defined professionalism as performing at a constant, despite distractions. Each diverse setting in life is fraught with distraction, and often, adding to the stress of unexpected situations, there are people over-reacting due to unrealistic expectations that things are going to develop according to their own preferred styles or plans. Wouldn't it be great if people would just follow the humorous advice of the bumper sticker: "Save time. See it my way!" All of us would like people to see things our way, but that's not the way of the world.

In every environment, it is usual to find people whose styles, ideas, perceptions, and personalities clash. One person may thrive on improvisation, while another embraces established protocols. One may prefer a silent, focused workplace, while another enjoys working while visiting with a co-worker and music playing in the background. These differences can, at times, preface larger disagreements involving greater issues.

If we examine our various workplaces, we can probably think of a person or two with styles opposite ours, and with whom we have had an open conflict once or twice. Sometimes when these opposite styles collide, work progress slows or halts. When we run into conflict, our human nature compels us to find someone to bond with who shares our own views, to feel affirmed that we are seeing things the right way. It is precisely these times of distraction that test our credentials as professionals.

When we come to expect distractions, such as interruptions, differing viewpoints, clashing styles, etc., we prepare and equip ourselves to more effectively pursue organizational and team goals. All of us can pave the way for dealing with complicated decisions involving sure-to-come unforeseen developments, by encouraging thought and input from our diverse ranks regarding future goals. By granting advance opportunities for involvement, we are investing in potential buy-in from our team members, who are all seeing things from different angles. Inviting conflict during preliminary planning of a new process better prepares teams to function smoothly during the crucial time of implementation.

Different people seeing different things in different ways is nothing different. It's life. Professionals address these occurrences as minor distractions. They stay focused on big pictures and team goals, and are always finding a constant at which to perform.

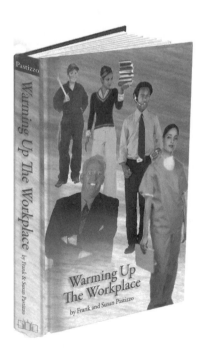

3

SELF-AWARENESS

1

The Person in Front of You

"Work is love made visible. And if you cannot work with love but only with distaste, it is better that you should leave your work and sit at the gate of the temple and take alms of those who work with joy."—Kahlil Gibran

At the counter of a convenience store once, I apparently was annoying the clerk just by being there. I think summer help season had started and this young teenager was faced with the sigh-full burden of listening to me, figuring out what I needed, giving it to me, taking my money for it, and giving me change. When I asked for some extra quarters for the parking meter, her eyes rolled to a degree proportionate to having asked her to mow the lawn with a push mower. She seemed totally in a hurry to get rid of me so she could return to her seat and continue to hate being there.

While this was clearly one of the most obvious and over-the-top exhibitions of how some find being at work distasteful, there are other, milder attitudes that people employ to show they are not happy when placed in the role of service provider.

I find it is always worth the attempt to try to connect with the person in front of you, no matter which side of the service counter you're standing on.

If we respond to our initial defense mechanisms and match or even escalate the distasteful tone, we effectively lower ourselves to the same level we find distasteful in others. This tactic might make us feel better for the moment, but does nothing to alleviate the underlying problem. A curt or sarcastic response, whether aimed at a preoccupied teen, a disgruntled adult, or anyone in between, just makes the atmosphere even more hostile. Instead, an offering of empathy ... "Will you get to have any time off today?...", or "Sorry, you seem to be having a really tough day..." may just bring out an appreciative smile, or a small bit of friendly conversation. When people feel validated, often they feel freed up to examine their own countenance and the possible negative effect it is having on those around them. Often, this may be enough to have them "tune up" their demeanor and turn the exchange into a good-humored one.

Some might ask "Why should I make the effort to be nice when someone is acting like a jerk?" Because in improving the environment, we are making things more pleasant for everyone, including ourselves, the person in front of us, and for those that will follow. Rather than simply saying, "Have a nice day," we have taken a few simple steps to try to create one.

2

HURTFUL HUMOR

"Remember not only to say the right thing in the right place, but far more difficult still, to leave unsaid the wrong thing at the tempting moment."—Benjamin Franklin

When a group of people get together and converse about anything, for some there is often another agenda lying just below the surface: to be funny. There is an emotionally empowering reward for the person who comes up with the spontaneous quip or zinger or barb that makes the others laugh. Having been a comedian my entire life, I thrive on the reinforcing encouragement of laughter. Some say that timing is everything. It's not. Timing is certainly important, but appropriateness trumps.

Don Imus's radio and television show was an edgy form of entertainment designed to bring current events into a forum of class clowns, where the tone varied between serious discussion and ridicule of people in the public eye. When Don and his sidekick Bernard got going, their competing momentums frequently resulted in titillating tirades laden with racist, sexist, sacrilegious, and vulgar expression. For some, it was daring stuff in our age of political correctness, likened to the excitement and apprehension of a classroom when the bad kid in the back of the room is called upon to read his original poetry. Don Imus's show was at times a personification of a Little Johnny joke. It was the character he played, and people wanted to hear what he would say next and also wanted to see and hear the reaction of his show's guests from the establishment, such as Senator John McCain, Andrea Mitchell, Tim Russert, etc.

Imus kept some credibility over the years because he mostly stayed serious when he was discussing current events with his guests. He reserved derisive banter to moments with his cronies, while guests and viewers could remain removed and thus not seem to be associated or tainted. In fact, many of us get into small groups and make fun of friends and loved ones with all sorts of non-flattering imitations of exaggerated traits. We do not broadcast these less-than-respectful moments to the world at large; instead, we keep them within some small circle of people who identify with and appreciate the comedy. We may engage in impromptu dialogue and get caught up in a moment trying to fashionably emulate some famous entertainer's style like Chris Rock, Larry the Cable Guy, or Jeff Foxworthy, and sometimes the character we are playing overtakes our own best intentions, and we may go over a line and become hurtful.

To consciously try to instill humor in a work setting has to be a thoughtful process. The captive audience is there for economic reasons. It is not a nightclub or an Andrew Dice Clay concert. Reenacting a scene from Borat or Jackass is probably best reserved for a selected audience in private. Some jokes or comic styles will inevitably hurt people, and people have a civil right to a workplace free of such hurtful moments. Yes, we live in a free country and have the right to free speech, but when we are at work, we represent the companies we work for, and what we say or do becomes what the company is saying and doing. Don Imus was a syndicated, national airwaves entertainer and was paid $10 Million per year by CBS. He went over the line many times and had been called on the carpet enough to warrant his firing. While his show was clearly successful and certainly entertaining, our national media have declared that social appropriateness trumps. I hope for consistency in this stance and that all of our mainstream airwaves become more active in their non-tolerance of hurtful broadcasting. Publicly expressing mean things and openly degrading people causes hurt, alienation, and resentment. If *we the people* were to systematically allow such hurtful broadcasts in our nation's mass communications, we would likely see more hurt, alienated, and resentful individuals taking irresponsible and vengeful retaliations against our public. Open societies should not antagonize their masses.

There will always be select nightclubs and cable channels and live concerts in our free society that offer a forum for alternative and edgy expression, but a line in the sand has been drawn here. When we are in public, or at work, or have access to the public masses, we are tasked to maintain a measured amount of civility and respect to preserve human dignity. This is true social progress.

Avoiding the Turn Off

Nature is oblivious to reputation.
We redefine ourselves by how we act next.

"We have two ears and one mouth so that we can listen twice as much as we speak."—Epictetus

Outside an airport newsstand by a departure gate once, I struck up a conversation with a rancher from Montana, who had just returned from a family vacation in Hawaii. He raised beef and grain, and while most of his contemporaries had begun to use four-wheel ATV's, he used only horses to oversee his cattle and land. Even though he was proudly sporting a Hawaiian shirt, I could, for a moment, only see the cowboy and felt in awe to be in his company. I asked him about his family. My dad told me once, to get on the good side of others, encourage them to talk about themselves. He mentioned his son, who had a degree in geology, but had come home to work the ranch. He said there wasn't much opportunity to make money if you were young and living in Montana. I now wish I had pursued this line of questioning. Instead, I asked him if he or his son used the Internet. He admitted he was computer illiterate. I recommended researching how they could pursue some sort of cottage industry. I went on to say how it has begun to matter less and less where we live, because the marketplace is so accessible through computers. I even went into some specifics on how I was able to find certain investment items on e-bay and how they could be resold for substantial profit...I wish this would have been one of those times when I had been just a listener. I saw it in his eyes... that glaze that comes when your topic is no longer appealing... the *turn off*. He mumbled a few more pleasantries..."that's interesting, isn't that something..." and wandered back to the waiting area to join his family. While my topic had been very interesting to me, and perhaps many others, I had failed to appreciate who he was, how my topic alienated him, and I missed an opportunity to learn more of his life and values.

Managing our communication styles and taking care in how we listen and respond are cornerstones of relationships, and it is so very easy and common to make mistakes. In many instances, communication is so one-sided the *turn-off* is not even noticed. Some years back, I went through "training" where, like seals at Seaworld, we were to learn how to balance seven habits on our noses. While I embraced many of the ideas, especially the ideas of emotional deposits and withdrawals, many of us in the class were *turned off* by the pervasive **business and sales** spin of the company representative, the canned lesson plans, and the seemingly paranoid trade marking™ of every catchy phrase. *First things first*™. *Begin with the end in mind*™. It became clear that these good ideas had become commodities for sale and we were the customers and we needed these products to improve our lives, **but wait, there's more**, if you subscribe to their principles now, they will give you this nice binder to anchor yourself to for the next year for only $49.95! One of the principles teaches us that we should feel there is an abundance of wealth and goodness and we should celebrate the achievements of others and take comfort in our faith that goodness and wealth will come our way too. We should not feel threatened by others' achievements or overly protective of our own assets. We should share. They call this *Abundance Mentality*™ ... but it's trade marked!!, so nobody *steals* it.

I am sure I could have absorbed more good ideas had I not felt insulted by the arrogance of the company's style and sales pitch. Perhaps if they had made more emotional deposits with their audience, we would have been more inclined to listen and would have not turned off in such a hurry. Here are a few of life's lessons I continue to learn: we must not *can* our communication with individuals but instead find ways to make it authentic and spontaneous. We need to be real listeners and adapt our styles to different people to avoid the *turn-off*. Don't try to sell computer culture to a horseman from Montana.

4

Human Competencies

"Travel is fatal to prejudice, bigotry, and narrow-mindedness, and many of our people need it sorely on these accounts. Broad, wholesome, charitable views of men and things cannot be acquired by vegetating in one little corner of the earth all one's lifetime."—Mark Twain

One of the benefits of speaking around the country is having many opportunities to sit down with professionals from all walks of life, and have really good conversations regarding life, family, jobs, etc. Last week we had just finished a keynote presentation for the Ohio Hospital Association in Columbus, and I had an opportunity to converse with an old friend and colleague, who had been in the audience. He commented on one part of our message that encourages people to go beyond the golden rule, e.g., treating others as *you* like to be treated and instead, stretching ourselves to attempt to treat others as *they* like to be treated. He went on to praise the advice we give: to willingly modify our own behaviors to attempt to be more appealing to others, and said that we might consider elaborating on this point, and presenting on topics of Diversity and Cultural Competencies.

I was not very familiar with the term Cultural Competencies and had to ask him to explain. He informed me how public agencies, especially hospitals and health centers, are striving to be more inclusive of different cultures by ensuring there are multi-language signs in their hallways, interpreters on staff, and making many other attempts to see that our public institutions are more familiar-feeling to many. He also spoke of pending legislation that will make these Cultural Competencies required for agencies receiving Medicare and other types of governmental funding. It was gratifying to realize that our work in this area has been a little ahead of the curve.

As we spoke more I told him of one of my Diversity presentations at an IBM plant six years ago and how eclectic their cafeteria was. The cuisine was truly international with choices of sushi, falafel, couscous, curries, enchiladas, pasta, salads, etc. These are tangible efforts to create an environment in a workplace for people to feel included. They show the willingness to make overtures of human connection—to show receptiveness and respect—our best stuff.

The willingness to explore and learn languages of those we live and work among is a true demonstration of cultural competency for all of us. Policies that advocate for a national language standard seem intolerant and unnecessary. Insisting that, in the workplace, others completely drop their native cultures and languages in favor of some type of homogenized, efficient manner is saying that people cannot be themselves when they are at work. It prevents people from doing their best work. It accentuates an *us and them* environment. This keeps us insulated from a whole range of ideas and solutions that can come from a more global outlook, many of which don't even translate into our corporate culture. We cannot stay in one little corner of the earth, even if we want to. Travel, actual and virtual, is now inescapable in this world-wide web we live in. Diversity is life, and broadening ourselves to connect with others is what makes us all competent as humans and more productive in our lives together.

5

A KIND MIRROR

"If indeed you must be candid, be candid beautifully."—*Kahlil Gibran*

Recently, in the midst of a twenty-four day, fifteen-show tour of five states, one of our hosts had us presenting for a large group of community members in a school gymnasium. Our two-hour Warm Up The Workplace program is a pretty complex mix of philosophy, stories, theatre, stand-up comedy, live music, and audience participation. It has a distinct order, and is quite dependent on a rhythm of delivery to be effective. Each transition sets up the next so that it fits together into a holistic stage experience for the audience.

The first interruption came in the way of a young woman who was asking the group around her for a pen and paper to write down a few notes; this created quite a stir, with the five or six people around her looking in purses and pockets, while those around them were curious as to what was happening. I stopped and asked what she needed, pretty much to let her know she was causing quite a distraction. A little while later, a student entered the gym from the far left and asked the audience to pass a message to her father, who was seated on the far right. Like a "wave cheer," I watched the message get passed and saw many break their focus to observe the passing. I stopped the presentation and asked who the message was for, and we notified the dad, who exited the gym. A moment later, a young mother attempted to quiet her tiny newborn in the third row. I tried to let her know that she did not need to worry and that her baby was welcome to make as much noise as he needed, but it turns out, I was too late in demonstrating tolerance. My exasperation from the other interruptions had already surfaced and set another, unfortunate tone, and even my attempt to extend reassurance was interpreted by some as being sarcastic.

I found this out several days later, half a continent away. Our host from the gymnasium was able to catch us on our cell phone and give us priceless counsel. She began with a list of positive feedback she had received from many, but then thought she should let me know that several people had mentioned they had felt I'd been somewhat severe with the minor interruptions and had shown some snappiness within a program designed to foster kindness.

For the graceful manner in which my new-found friend imparted this information, and the obvious value of it in my career's endeavor to encourage warmth, I am grateful beyond words. Thank you for your warmth and honesty and for being such a kind mirror. Since our phone conversation, I have had numerous interruptions and new opportunities to practice a polite pause, with maybe an explanation of not wanting to lose my place. For the note taker and dad in the gym, I am really, really sorry for the embarrassment I must have caused you.

There are many instances when we will all be dependent on friends to let us know that we might have behaved in a manner inconsistent with our best intentions. When they hold up their kind mirrors, we need to take care to accept these valuable offerings. Life's interruptions are a constant, and most of our stress comes from an unrealistic expectation that things are going to go as *we* plan. I am glad that I am now better equipped to deal with the countless human surprises that are sure to occur. Thanks again.

6

PUBLIC CORRECTNESS
A Matter of Respect

*"I have noticed that nothing I have never said ever did me any harm."—
Calvin Coolidge*

On the eve of our country's presidential elections, many of us become more and more vocal with our loyalties, our issues, and our emotions. It is precisely at these times when we need to remember that we are in a workplace with diverse people making a living to support themselves and their families. People at work are a captive audience, and none of us should feel free to expound upon our personal viewpoints in this environment. To do so risks offending or even deeply upsetting another and disrupting what should be a positive focus.

Reserving the expression of political, sexual, and religious viewpoints for private conversations with like-minded associates is always the best rule, and even these moments really should be minimized when we are in the workplace. This is something we, along with many others, have learned from going over the line and saying more than we should in a public place, when we should have remained respectful of people's differences.

Throughout the Academy Award-winning movie Forrest Gump, Tom Hanks' character was one who simply and objectively went through time making contributions during huge, historical events.

He seemed to just be there, while trying to be loyal to his friends and doing what was asked of him. In one clever and delicately directed moment of the film, Forrest was asked to say a few words about Vietnam in front of the Lincoln Memorial in Washington, D.C. There he stood in uniform in front of thousands of people in the film, and millions of captive moviegoers around the world. Here's the point: there is nothing Forrest Gump could have said that would not have been controversial or upsetting to someone. Out of respect for the audience and to maintain the positive momentum of the character and the film, Forrest's microphone was unplugged and none of us were able to hear his views.

From time to time when certain topics arise in our workplaces, we need to protect the positive momentum of others, as well as ourselves, and out of respect and loyalty to our companions, gladly unplug our own microphones.

7

REMAINING STEADY

Each of us is tasked to complete our daily schedules and honor our commitments to those around us. The complexity of these commitments is astounding. With our work and home and families, all of us can be spread pretty thin. At times we even feel a need to vent our schedules to each other! It helps us to put order to our lives. We tell one another what we have to complete. It's rehearsal and it helps us feel supported . . . and then there will always come a time when in the middle of an extremely complex agenda, each of us will be thrown some sort of surprise thing. We will have to juggle our deadlines, change our rehearsed schedule, and find a way to press on.

Remaining steady is a constant task that we need to keep imminent. It needs to be at the top of our list: "I am not going to let a surprise or shock push me to a point beyond my control where I speak or act harshly toward those around me." That being said, because we are human, we know we will not always be able to be successful with this task. There will be times when we find ourselves losing control. That's when we need to re-form and quickly take responsibility for impeding the positive momentum around us and apologize for any grief we have caused.

Further, we need to be aware that those around us are subject to these same human traits, and that the tasks and surprising developments set upon all of us create intensities and passions.

Remaining steady in the face of unexpected developments is a worthwhile goal of any team. We should always be working to improve our instincts and try to know when our colleagues are at their wit's end. We can try to lighten their loads. We should ensure we do not chide them for any loss of control; rather, we strive to preserve their dignity, avoid their embarrassment, help them recover their balance, and as a matter of course, welcome their return to the team.

8

Pathfinders

'You can complain because roses have thorns, or you can rejoice because thorns have roses."—Ziggy, character in comic strip by Tom Wilson

My friend for life, Larry, shared one of his life's lessons with me recently. He and his new wife lived in Saratoga Springs, NY, and their apartment was in a nice, renovated hotel in the city center. Because of its location, their parking lot was frequently used by city center visitors, even though it was reserved for tenants. During one of northern New York's winter blizzards, Larry came home from work and had to circle his block several times, waiting for a car to exit his full parking lot. The roads were a mess and the snowplows were plowing the street, and right after a car had left the lot, a snowplow passed and left a deep snow bank across the parking lot entrance. Larry made a run through it, but became hung up, with half of his car sticking out in the street.

Totally stressed, and with the elevator out of order, he headed up the stairs to gather his new bride to help him drive the car, so he could push it out of the snow. As he told this story, Larry shared with me a key element of what would become a transforming moment: he had the presence of mind to realize that his wife was totally oblivious to his last fifteen minutes of searching and waiting for a parking space and getting stuck in a snow bank, and he decided not to unload his stress on her. Instead, he just asked her if she could come out for a moment and help him move the car, while he pushed it out of the snow.

On their way through the parking lot, his new bride put her arm in his and asked, "After we finish with the car, can we go for a walk? It's pretty out."

Larry says that was all it took for him to forget all about the stress and anger he was experiencing the moment before. He says at that moment he felt like the luckiest and richest person on earth.

That scenario could have been reversed by even a slight change in reactions and behaviors. We all have the power to do what Henry David Thoreau calls *elevating our lives through conscious endeavor*, or more simply put, doing good things on purpose. There will always be a steady stream of uexpected phenomena in all of our lives. Some of it may initially cause our blood to boil, but with just a little bit of foresight, we can discover new ways to react and more pleasant paths to follow. We do have the power to transform ourselves and how we are going to feel next.

Larry's concern for the feelings of another kept him purposeful and restrained and allowed the moment to transform rather than projecting and dictating foulness. I am grateful to my friend for sharing his insight and warmth with me, and I'm going for a walk soon. It's pretty out.

9

I Already Knew That

"I love to learn, but I am not always ready to be taught." —Winston Churchill

During our presentations, we demonstrate the difficulties and pressures involved when learning new tasks, especially when others are watching. The scenario develops like this: a volunteer comes to the front of the audience to learn how to juggle. After a few basic steps, I can usually have a person juggling three scarves or plastic shopping bags in about a minute and a half. Often, the person is amazed at how quickly he or she has learned. We mostly find that nearly the entire audience has attempted to juggle before, but once greeted with their own, initial ineptness, quit their attempt to learn.

Quitting our attempts to learn something new seems to be related to our avoidance of appearing incompetent to ourselves and others. We try to preserve our dignities and status by not displaying our lack of skills, experience, or knowledge. We like to appear competent, experienced, and knowledgeable, sometimes to the point of feigning indifference when we are truly surprised by some new development, as if to say, "I already knew that." We may then even move on to someone else and relay the new development in the hope that that person shows surprise, so we can experience some feelings of influence and power. Human behavior sure can be a bit weird sometimes.

Those who step forward to learn something new, admitting a bit of ignorance, are the quickest studies. Those who are preoccupied with preserving their own status are the slowest, and often leave learning situations with incomplete skill sets, but will mask this incompleteness masterfully.

Allowing yourself to be visibly influenced by another endears you to that other. Becoming a student, entering new territories, and being surprised by developments is an exciting way to go through life. The next time you find yourself acting unmoved and uttering (or at least thinking) "I know" to everything another tells you, see if you can find some way to turn it around and say, "I don't think I would have seen that coming," or "That sounds like a better way to do it," and watch how encouraged the speaker becomes to tell you more.

How to Juggle Three Plastic Shopping Bags

1. Start with one hand and two bags. Do not wad up the bags. When they are open, they float.

2. Keeping your hand upside down, grip one bag with your index finger and thumb, and the other with your remaining three fingers.

3. Toss one bag straight up in front of you, about two feet above your head.

4. When that bag begins its descent, toss the other bag up the same way and grab the first bag which has now dropped to about face level, and throw it back to the top.

5. Keep doing this process with one hand until you can exchange bags four times without dropping. (You are playing catch with gravity.)

6. Now repeat entire process with your other hand.

7. After you have mastered one hand-two bag juggling on both sides, you are ready for three bags with two hands.

8. Hold two bags with one hand as in #2 above. Hold the third bag with the other hand.

9. Toss up first of two bags with one hand, as it starts to descend, toss up second bag with same hand, and catch first bag with same hand.

10. As the second bag begins its descent, toss up third bag with other hand and catch second bag with that hand, and continue process one side at a time, toss catch, toss catch, toss catch.

11. You're juggling! But you already knew that.☺

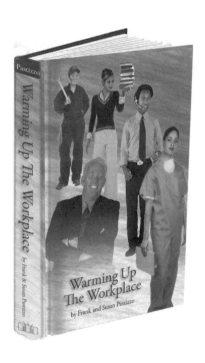

Warming Up
The Workplace

by Frank and Susan Pastizzo

4

COMMUNICATING

1

The Shut Down

People shut down when they've had their feelings hurt. Their affect becomes flat and protective and they often retreat into silence and avoid interaction altogether. Sometimes they become sarcastically animated, or sternly sharp and cutting. When feelings have been hurt with any frequency, these protective devices become prevalent in people's general demeanors, especially when they are around those who have hurt them or those they do not know well enough to place trust in. When in a group environment such as a school or work setting, where their communication is routinely required, their confidence levels are at a low, and they need to be shown that they can again trust the people within these environments not to hurt them again. Chances are they are not going to be shown this.

Because many of us have been hurt before, we display guardedness in our various public encounters. We try to keep our feelings out of it. In the film Cinderella Man, the actor Bruce McGill, playing the real-life boxing promoter Jimmy Johnston, responds to the sarcastic statement, "You're all heart," (when he had told contender James Braddock that he would not be offered a shot at the title) by saying this: "My heart is for my family. My brains and my *guts* are for business, and this is business."

And there we have it... this separation of our sincere and feeling lives from our at-work lives: the keeping of our feelings out of it-- the turning off of our empathies. When we shut down our own feelings, we are unequipped to connect with the feelings of others, and more and more, our workplaces, the places where we spend the most of our waking hours, become dehumanized. We function in cold, calculating, and calloused ways. We may reserve our kindly selves for a select few, but our in-with-the-group behavior stays on guard.

Of course these paragraphs reflect extremes, and of course, for the sake of making our workplaces safer for people, many of us overcome the tendency to shut down and still share our kindly ways in spite of those hurtful moments. Doing so requires a certain strength and maturity which is absolutely required of those in leadership positions, and needs to be fostered in everyone else. *Keeping it warm* goes a long way towards preventing the shut down.

2

PROBLEMS WITH PROTOCOL

One of the concepts in the film **What The Bleep Do We Know Anyway?** deals with the limitations of human consciousness. One limitation is our tendency to mostly only see what is already recognized. An example would be when we purchase a new type of automobile and then start noticing all of the other vehicles like ours when they drive by. Those cars were always passing by, but we did not notice them until we had familiarized ourselves with them. This same example holds true when we look up a new word in the dictionary and then notice it more and more frequently in our reading.

When we adopt a specific set of behaviors to address situational interactions with people, we enter into the present with an entire set of past-experience assumptions, and we end up treating a current circumstance as if it has already happened. To quote the script from the film mentioned above, "we treat today as if it's already yesterday." We put people and conversations and new events into frames and boxes based upon old events, and often, we remain only superficially involved, and unmoved, and treat each moment and person and interaction as commonplace. Consequently, we don't even notice much of what's happening around us (like when we did not notice those new cars or words), because we have not consciously familiarized ourselves with what is actually going on. Again, this is often a self-imposed limitation of human consciousness... a lot gets by each of us.

One of the problems with protocols is that we further limit ourselves by behaving in predetermined ways, thus contributing to our tendency to miss nuances of experience. Now this may be a very good thing when one is involved in driving a car or some other set of physical behaviors which require compliance to avoid catastrophes. However, when we treat people and our interactions like they are old hat, we miss wonderful opportunities to see things from new perspectives, gain different points of view, experience new levels of human fulfillment and joy, and gain valuable insights.

When someone begins interacting with us in a pre-determined way, we deflate immediately. Think of your own reactions to the sales pitch, the form letter, the background-chatter-filled phone call request for a minimum sponsorship to some, perhaps fraudulent, benevolent fund, the listing of voice mail menu selections, etc. When we are subjected to behaviors that are planned and canned, we feel manipulated. We feel that our own individualities are being dismissed, and that we are reduced from a valuable entity to just another name or number. In this state we are much less receptive to any further meaningful interaction—we just want to escape.

We need to stay as mindful as we can when we are interacting with those around us, whether we are the proponent or the recipient of some given protocol. If each of us could just try to open ourselves up a little more at the onset of each interaction, to be a bit more spontaneous, to listen holistically, and to be more cognizant of the spirit of the person in front of us ...we would be contributing much more toward each other's wisdom and joy, and all of us would know a little, or maybe a lot more.

3

SINCERITY VS. CLICHÉ

In the novel <u>1984</u>, by George Orwell, Newspeak was the officially sanctioned language. Updated manuals were released each year by the government to inform citizens of what new words and phrases were acceptable for common usage and which words were to be made obsolete and stricken from everyday speech. People who used outmoded language were corrected and sometimes fined. Behavior was dictated by an imposing, omnipresent screen, where Big Brother continuously fed the public information and guidance toward acceptable practices. This novel was written in 1948 and served as a cautionary piece for free citizens frightened of being manipulated by a tyrannical leadership.

Relative to the self-governance of our own behaviors, it's interesting to compare Orwell's dark vision from 1948 with the pervasive influence of television and film in our current times. Do we limit our own positive actions due to the subliminal or overt influence of what we see in the media?

Many of us like to be original. When something is broadcast it soon becomes old hat. When it's played over and over again, it is then taken out of our everyday lives by our own drive to remain original. Already, in 2008, we've been told the words and phrases that are no longer in. The problem is that we sometimes refrain from saying or doing exactly the right thing because it has already been said or done by someone else, or we are simply afraid of an onlooker's perception and some potential reaction we may get. One example is a phrase that was uttered once by one of our leaders. It became a sound bite and was played over and over again in the 1990's. It became part of comedy routines and can hardly be uttered anymore without evoking an eye roll and an assumption that one is joking, being insincere, or sarcastic. What is this mystery phrase? It displays consideration, concern, thought, and empathy perfectly, but we have eliminated it from our list of acceptable expressions because it has become corny from our media's overusage. The phrase we are referring to is, "I feel your pain."

With the pervasiveness of electronic media constantly rumbling in the foreground and background of our lives, we hope we do not become unconsciously chained by the media's dictation of what is "in" or outdated, or so fearful of an overused, hence unfashionable, sound bite, that we reflexively give up our opportunities to sincerely express ourselves, when we may need to the most. After all, we are our own Big Brothers, and we can speak from our hearts when we choose.

Why do some put the brakes on when they are about to extend kindness? Sometimes people will not do the right thing because they're afraid someone will think they're doing it for the wrong reasons. So rather than doing the right thing for the right reasons and risk the possibility of being misinterpreted, they take no action. What we say and what we do will always be interpreted by some people as being too nice, self serving, corny, over-the-top, cliché, or old hat. This doesn't matter. If the basis for an action is sincerity and kindness, it is the right thing to do. Sincerity never stops being original.

4

ONE PROBLEM
WITH PUPPY SITTING

I t was my idea to take Griffey for two weeks that summer. Sue and I love dogs, but our speaking and traveling schedule prohibits our owning one, so I jumped on the chance to have this four-month-old, Husky-Yellow Lab mix.

As we brought Griffey with us around town and to the lake, his number of admirers grew and people began to ask us how we would ever be able to give him back. We knew it would be hard, and it was not made easier with his leaping into our bed each morning to show us how happy he was to be starting a new day with us. We had to make a choice to either take people's advice and not get too attached or get as close as we could and enjoy our time with this awesome creature. We chose the latter, and loved each moment with our temporary family member. Needless to say, we had a very sad farewell. The choice was ours.

I find a lot of parallels with at-work relationships and how many people stay distant with their colleagues. Many guard against becoming too close with their coworkers for lots of stated reasons, e.g., prioritizing roles, recognition of authority, maintaining professional effectiveness, preserving rank and file traditions, etc., but I think one often unstated human motivation for detachment is the fear of loss and of having one's feelings hurt. If we avoid trusting and making friends with people we see everyday at work, or choose to categorize them as work friends, as opposed to authentic friends, we then feel safe. We have the convenience of not having much stock in how we behave toward one another. We can stay cool and act as if our workplace demeanor is separate from our authentic selves. Taken toward negative extremes, we can harbor grudges and behave immaturely, we can gossip, backstab, and manipulate. We can jump from clique to clique and group to group with no need for consistency. After all, this is our job; it's not our life. Even when someone temporarily blurs lines of workplace relationship boundaries by hosting an office holiday party in his private home, the brief familiarity can be mere superficial gloss, and it will only take a few days back in the office to return to our estranged normalcy.

One theme we often return to in these columns is that we spend more time at work than we do at home and that it makes perfect sense that our workplaces reflect the values we want in our lives. Examining our behavior and relationships with our coworkers to see if we demonstrate loyalty, honesty, and consistency can be an important first step toward making true friendships and enriching the quality of our lives. Small steps to show our willingness to become closer to one another can enhance all aspects of a company's performance and promote accountability at all levels. People perform better because they want to demonstrate how they care for one another.

Life itself is temporary. To go through it avoiding attachment can make it feel even more so. In each brief encounter it is possible to behave in ways that create a sense of closeness so authentic that it remains long after the moment passes. This is something we can keep permanently whether we are at home or at work. The choice is ours.

5

STEWARDS

"A human being is a part of the whole, called by us, "Universe," a part limited in time and space. He experiences himself, his thoughts and feelings as something separated from the rest -- a kind of optical delusion of his consciousness. This delusion is a kind of prison for us, restricting us to our personal desires and to affection for a few persons nearest to us. Our task must be to free ourselves from this prison by widening our circle of compassion to embrace all living creatures and the whole of nature in its beauty. Nobody is able to achieve this completely, but the striving for such achievement is in itself a part of the liberation and a foundation for inner security."—Albert Einstein

"With just a little witty skepticism we can kill a good deal of hope in a young person. Life is waiting everywhere, the future is flowering everywhere, but we only see a small part of it and step on much of it with our feet."—Hermann Hesse

Each of us in our lives has capabilities for heightened levels of awareness of how we affect and interact with the world around us. Sometimes we are lost in our own individual agendas, and sometimes we strive to combine energies, connecting with one another, trying to achieve some measure of human greatness in our services.

How do we measure greatness? Is it by the wealth we generate for ourselves or our companies? Is it how we apply this wealth to further enable and improve our services? Perhaps, but if we are striving for true greatness in our professions, we need to perpetually encourage, cultivate, and contribute toward each other's creativities and energies. What Einstein refers to as a delusion of consciousness can keep us from feeling connected to the rest, and may imprison us with feelings of self-doubt, unworthiness, and defensiveness. We may be inclined to withdraw, or ridicule, or convey some other kind of life extinguishing behavior. It is up to all of us to elevate our with-itness and to try to help one another get to and remain at peak levels of contribution.

When we climbed our first Adirondack High Peak, there was a volunteer of the Adirondack Mountain Club at the top. She was a Mountain Steward who was there to protect the fragile alpine plant life above 4,000 ft. She kept people from walking off the bedrock and trails. She was very respectful as she pointed out what many of us wouldn't have seen—the small things that took a lifetime to develop and that a careless footstep would have killed.

Each of us holds a similar stewardship in our workplaces, fragile environments also, where each of us brings our own sense of security and ability, focusing our attitudes and skills towards accomplishments. We have to avoid stepping on each other and strive to protect this venue of potential human greatness. It can bring rewards to all and help us celebrate many achievements together.

6

THE RIGHT PEOPLE

For ten years I managed facilities for a large, non-profit long-term care organization in upstate NY. One weekend while only a skeleton staff was on duty, an elderly woman called one of our nursing homes asking when her Meals-On-Wheels would be delivered. The CNA (Certified Nurse Aide) who answered the phone merely had to inform the woman that we did not provide that service on weekends, but instead she followed up on a feeling that something wasn't quite right, and engaged the woman in a conversation, asking her when she normally had her meals delivered. The woman did not know. She then asked where the woman lived. It turned out the woman was from a small city over 35 miles away, outside of our service area. Again, the CNA only needed to tell her she had called the wrong provider, and that we did not provide service to her area... but instead she delved a little deeper and found the woman to be disoriented. She got the woman's address and had a co-worker call that town's police department, who arrived while she was still talking on the phone. They found a dehydrated, malnourished, and very confused patient...

It turns out that the woman had been at a Senior Day a few weeks before and had picked up a free pen with our company's name and toll free number. She called that number, and she got the *right people.*

When I tell that story during my presentations there is always a moment of quiet that goes through the audience. Mostly, we all want to be the right people, I think. However, we often get so caught up in the rush of the numbers game that we leave some measure of quality aside.

Taking time to address individual needs and styles and to routinely look at our processes as a team from the perspectives of those most affected or from the end results, will always promote quality improvement. As managers, our goal is to achieve the best quality possible in our absence. We need to count on our employees to feel comfortable with their knowledge of their jobs, and to be able to spontaneously mold their service to fit the individual being served. Showing a customer that we recognize his or her individuality and that we will stretch ourselves to meet a specific need is the best neon glitz we can put on our businesses. These are the behaviors that build the kind of customer loyalties and connections that are seldom broken. These are the behaviors that demonstrate that we are the right people.

7

Taking a Pass

"Some people think it's all right to take a pass on being human."
—Robert Bertram, Tufts University

M y mom had surgery a couple of years back and had to have part of her lung removed after a small cancer was discovered. Our family waited four hours in the waiting room. The doctor came down from the operating room and walked over to my dad and asked him to please come with him. I walked with him and the doctor, who silently walked us down the hall and directed us into a small counseling room. He said, "Please, sit down and make yourself comfortable." My dad was quite shaken and let out a quivery, "Oh God," as he sat. The doctor then paused and said in a measured way, "The surgery went well and she's fine." Was the fifty-five seconds the doctor kept us on edge intended to keep us on edge? Was it a conscious relishing of the power he had over us or was he so far removed due to his technical concentration, that he had stopped feeling the connection to the emotional sensitivities of others? Did he feel that because of his surgical prowess he was somehow entitled to take a pass on being human?

A friend of mine told of his wife having emergency surgery for abdominal bleeding. One of her surgeons was passing his seat in a hallway after the operation. My friend asked, "Did everything go all right, Doc?" The doctor never broke stride, never replied, and after he had passed, from around ten feet away, with his back turned, raised an arm up in the air and gave a thumbs up gesture. When do people start to become so cold and indifferent? Is it related to rank and status? Would people find ways to regain some warmth and display compassion to one another if they realized they behaved this way?

Taking a pass on certain humanitarian behaviors comes with a lot of territories. Of course it is obvious to us that we need to make sure we are not using rank or power to manipulate people's emotions. But in addition, in the same way that some doctors may feel detached from the emotional levels of life that call for expressing sincerity and comforting manners, many higher ranking leaders practice the same aloofness with their subordinates and their subordinates' routines. Rank has its privileges, and some leaders often cannot bother themselves with the pesky details of running an office. They need to economize their attention-giving, and so things are done for them so they can remain focused on larger workings. Still, there are times when everyone needs to be mindful and give recognition to the people doing the mundane routines and show appreciation for those who make and keep everything functional. The best leaders know the names of the housekeepers and maintenance workers and clerical staff and purposefully show some understanding and appreciation of their routines and praise their efficiencies. Without the presence of this sincere kind of human touch, our workplaces remain at risk of becoming cold and detached, and high employee turnover will be a given.

There are times when we do not bother ourselves to interact with our coworkers. We all can make a mental note of our perceived aloofness and make it a priority to take time to stop and interact when we can take a moment. Being good company makes a good company. By not taking a pass, we are investing in the emotional stability of our group and keeping our people connected.

8

A USEFUL ENERGY

At five o'clock on Monday morning, January 5, 1998 it was around nine degrees Fahrenheit at the top of New York State, outside our home in Waddington, in the St. Lawrence River valley. It was nine degrees, and it was pouring rain. The ice was already so bad that tree limbs were down and electrical wires hung with thickening ice. Susan and I were beginning our day's preparation to drive to our teaching and healthcare jobs in the city of Ogdensburg, twenty miles to the west. We were looking outside at the frozen driveway when we saw a small fire ball arcing down the wires between telephone poles to the transformer at the top of a pole across the street. The transformer exploded with a shower of sparks and flashes and an incredible bang. We actually heard the electrical buzz come back through the wires into our house. The light above our dining room table surged with power and brightness, and then we lost power. The Ice Storm of 1998 had begun.

For more than 80 hours, steady freezing rain and drizzle fell over an area of several thousand square miles of eastern Ontario including Ottawa and Kingston, an extensive area in southern Quebec, northern New York, and parts of Vermont, New Hampshire, and Maine. Many power lines broke and over 1,000 pylons collapsed in chain reactions under the weight of the ice, leaving more than 4 million people without electricity. For the next week, our routines were gone. Schools were closed, so Susan, a teacher, focused her efforts on keeping our home lit and warm and turning it into a shelter for our other family members who lived close by.

The roads were closed except to essential personnel. As a health facility manager I was one of many deemed essential. Our company managed thirty-three health care facilities in thirteen communities. We had 800 employees and many people who counted upon us for our services. Our smaller health facilities were without power and some of our clients, other health center residents, and many people from their own homes were being evacuated and given cots in make-shift shelters in schools, colleges, fire houses, municipal buildings, and church basements. Nearly everyone shared a sense of urgency. We stood side-by-side with National Guardsmen and shoveled snow and ice off of roofs, we delivered meals, we helped people eat, we escorted elderly and disabled residents to school-gym locker-room toilets, and we tried to help people not feel stressed. Over the next week, in addition to the necessities, we also brought in hair dressers, musicians, and many volunteer companions. And even in the midst of crisis and uncertainty, there was such a presence of people being their best and brightest selves, that these shelters exemplified community stability. No matter what the circumstances, in each village I traveled to, there was the presence of this confidence and efficiency and the true warmth which comes from people getting together and helping people.

Now, over a decade later, it's our hope that a lot of people will sense this true warmth in their lives and feel assured of this same community focus and support. We hope people will reach out a little more, during times of stability as well as crisis, and find ways to demonstrate their connections. It's a good and useful energy to pass on.

9

THE WILLINGNESS TO BE WOUNDED

"Sometimes when we are generous in small, barely detectable ways it can change someone else's life forever."—Margaret Cho

One of our previous columns was entitled "The Shutdown" and discussed how people turn their feelings off after being hurt, to avoid being emotionally involved in certain interactions, because it would risk their being hurt again. The key point was that when we shut down our own feelings, we are unequipped and disabled when it comes to dealing with another's feelings.

In the September 18, 2005 issue of the New York Times, Dr. Abraham Verghese, of the University of Texas Health Sciences Center in San Antonio, wrote of his experience as a physician volunteering among the refugees of Hurricane Katrina. He spoke of putting his armor on to steel himself, much as he had done in his days of working shifts in the I.C.U.

In the process of treating people, he began asking each patient where they had spent their last five days and started to understand how they needed him to ask. He spoke of how it reminded him of his previous work in field clinics in India and Ethiopia, and how with so few medical resources, it was the careful listening, the thorough exam, and the laying on of hands that was the therapy.

He recounted an interaction he had had with one man who had managed to retain his dignity, even though he had lost his independence, and had spent two nights after the floods perched on a window ledge which was so narrow, his legs dangled in the water. The man had shared how his hopes had soared when he had seen Air Force One fly over, but had waited and waited and no help had come. The man had told him, "Doc, they treat refugees in other countries better than they treated us." Dr. Verghese listened, and then, sincerely told the man, "I'm so sorry. So sorry." Even though he had felt that his words sounded weak and inadequate, the man thanked him and told him he had needed to hear that.

A concept we revisit often is the importance of making ourselves truly available, and in the closing sentences of his article he beautifully expresses it. He has granted us permission to use his words here.

"I was still troubled by him when he left...this encounter had been carried to all the fullness that was permitted, and yet it (felt) incomplete. Driving home, I remembered my own metaphor of strapping on armor for the night shift. The years have shown that there is no armor. There never was. The willingness to be wounded may be all we have to offer."

CHERISH

by Frank Pastizzo

Exploring ways to warm up our living and working places.

"You will cherish this essential wisdom, delivered with warmth and wit."

Michael Brandwein,
Speaker/Author, *Training Terrific Staff* and
Super Staff Super Vision

"CHERISH presents clear, concise, and sound principles for living and working. Every manager and worker would do well to read and heed this book."

Dean Shrock, Ph.D.,
Author of *Doctor's Orders: Go Fishing*

"In his natural, direct style, Frank presents six simple, concrete concepts you can use to make a difference in your work environment. I encourage you to read on — CHERISH life — and go warm up your workplace!"

Margie Ingram, Vice President,
The Humor Project

"Frank Pastizzo writes a charming little book about how to be a 'Mensh', which is Yiddish for the essence of the human being. In a no-nonsense style he tells us ways we can 'menshify' our workplaces, our communities, and ultimately our planet."

Hedy Schleifer, M.A.,
International lecturer, workshop presenter
and trainer and author of *Sacred Choices*

"This book is filled with words of wisdom and inspiration which will positively guide our actions and prompt us to introspect and examine our behavior. It opens our eyes to what is meaningful in our daily lives and allows us to be who we are and to let others see us as we are...a book written from the heart, certain to touch yours."

Dr. Anjali Misra, Professor and Chair,
Teacher Education Department,
State University of New York

CHERISH

CHERISH

Frank Pastizzo

Warm Up the Workplace

Saranac Lake
New York

Dedication

This book is dedicated to the memory of Karen Lottie Bogardus. You animated yourself for everyone at all levels. When I think of North Country warmth, I'll always remember you. You *shot from the hip*, but were armed only with maple syrup and love.

Acknowledgements

A world of thanks is due to my wife, Susan, for her life's dedication to me and for her help with the writing of this book and her keen editing eye. I also thank my daughters and my original family for their unconditional love and support. One final thank you to my past employer, *United Helpers*, in Ogdensburg, New York, for giving me the opportunity to grow in one of the best human service provider agencies in the world. The people working there are true heroes!

Introduction

Mom used to pack my sisters off to school each morning. I wasn't old enough to go to school, but she would still make a brown-bag lunch and write "Frankie" on it, and I would go to "pretend school" under our upright piano. I would put my arm around one of her legs as she played hymns from church and Moon River. I would hold her leg as she pressed and released the sustain pedal. I would quietly eat my pb&j sandwich and press my face against the cabinetry of the piano and hear and feel the vibrations. This was my first school, and it was good to be included in the routine of the day. My mother surrounded my life with music, books and affection.

Dad was the passionate Italian. He was an authority figure—the school principal, the mayor. But most importantly he was the clown...the king of laughter. Even when admonishing, he had that special talent of calculating the precise length of time to let me stew in shame before enacting some self-effacing behavior to elicit a smile or chuckle from me, thus showing his own fallibility, managing our relationship, and preserving our lifetime connection. He assured me of my worth and his unconditional love.

Dr. William Glasser* writes of human beings requiring a sense of belonging, power, freedom and fun, in order to be fulfilled. These senses were prevalent in my early years, and the environment of my early childhood was a culture plate for the growth of emotional intelligence.

With my parents' divorce and my subsequent uprooting and transplanting into

*Choice Theory: A New Psychology of Personal Freedom; William Glasser, MD (See recommended reading list)

community after community, came my years of being a transient outsider. With the loss of belonging came the growth of defensiveness. With the loss of belonging came alienation and anti-social cynicism...the classic "I'm not okay and you're not okay". With the loss of belonging came detachment, distrust, hostility, self-absorption and the kind of broken-hearted disenchantment that can make a child say and do hateful things and feel inwardly satisfied that he has caused another to truly feel his pain.

Luckily, I had the roots I did. Without them I would not have been aware of the warmth I lacked and needed during my years of being an outsider. Without the belonging, power, freedom and fun prevalent in the initial years, I would not have had the expectations that things should be better. And it was the foundation laid during those years that allowed me to recognize my detachment and my perpetuation of callousness. Those formative years created who I am and how I feel. And it is those same formative years that now help me to recognize the in-disputable coldness that is so apparent in many of our dysfunctional workplaces of today.

This little book offers a simple acronym: CHERISH. It is amusing how I came to use an acronym. I had been doing presentation upon presentation in New York State on warming up our workplaces, relaxing our clinical countenances, promoting fun and downplaying stiff professionalism, when some of my peers, who had attended many "cutting-edge" presentations, suggested that I develop an acronym to help leave a last-ing impression. I had just seen a film in which a morally corrupt inspirational presenter's condescending treatment of his audience was accentuated by the use of a canned acronym. I inwardly laughed at how hackneyed it was. But in spite of how cliché it seemed, I came up with my acronym, which, ironically, was then viewed by my peers with some distaste due to its overt emotional context, but still I tried it a couple of times. It was accepted, though I sensed my audiences were aware that I had not truly embraced it. I then modified it a bit after accepting some suggestions from audience members who came up to speak with me after presentations. What has evolved is a simple list of words that *call* for actions and *illegalize* one specific action.

Overview

The acronym and simple philosophy
follow here:

C *Connect*

H *Humanize*

E *Emote*

R *Recognize*

I *Illegalize (a new word)*

S *Snapping*

H *Harmonize*

That's it. **CHERISH**. Work on these things in your every-day interactions, and you will find that your relationships, your home, office, school, hospital, organization, corporation, facility, plant, factory, or what have you, will become more respectful and consequently more functional.

When we **Connect**, we downplay status, and rank and file behaviors, which promote alienation, detachment, distrust, *us and them* mentalities, and divisiveness.

When we **Humanize**, we become tolerant of mistakes and allow each other our shortcomings. We build teams that focus on strengths.

This action is preferable to depending upon people who are pretending to be perfect, who hide errors, and are quick to be defensive to ensure their mistakes are never discovered, at any cost. Even at the cost of failure of an entire system or organization, some people are determined to remain fault-less.

When we **Emote**, we allow animation and play and expression and discovery. These qualities provide a much preferred and more creative environment than one which promotes stoicism and a jaded, nothing surprises me, business as usual, been there done that environment, which discourages expression and input for fear of appearing naïve. With a *business only, stiff upper lip, assembly line, Orwellian, on the clock* environment, we can kiss creativity good-bye and be assured that we will not reach our optimum levels of human output.

Recognize means recognition. Give it. Accept it. Say it. Don't conceal it. Don't withdraw it. Don't withhold it. Write it. Speak it. Put it on banners no matter how ordinary.

Illegalize Snapping: Humans snap. Crack that whip. Get people to jump. Make it snappy! Nothing causes more detriment and breeds more resentment than a Simon or Simone who imposes marching to a slave galley's drummer. These people have some inward need to control output in a manner only they and the few like them can recognize and appreciate, and with their insistent, hop-to, drill sergeant manner, make an entire system shut down. No one says or does anything for fear of their wrath, and nothing gets done, and although nothing gets done, to Simon and Simone's satisfaction, it doesn't get done in a very *orderly* manner. These people need to either reform, work alone or be let go.

Harmonize. The team is here. We call the shots. We have input and decide who works here. We keep rowing and celebrating all of our little victories and comforting each other and encouraging each other to do better when we at times fall short of the mark. We accept and embrace our diversity and know we have:

1. The right people to get the job done as well as or better than anyone else.

2. The right people to spend the most significant parts of our days with.

3. Done our best and feel proud we have positively affected people's lives.

I have written this book to offer a little bit of advice on structuring environments, and to give recognition to the heroes in our workplaces who pursue true visions of excellence in the face of archaic and dysfunctional systems. These true visions of excellence always stem from an ability to recognize when existing **habits** prohibit humanness. Statements like "We don't do it that way here…" and "In accordance with policy…" or "She will have to wait like everyone else…" are vexations to people with vision. People with vision embrace flexibility and bristle at the insistence of habits that govern behavior. They recognize that many endorse habits and rituals to such a degree, they lose sight of the purpose for which those habits were initiated. Habits are initiated to optimize best practices; people with vision recognize that *and* allow for individual variations with hopes for transcendence, progress and evolving best practices. They look for ways to appeal to the individual needs of people. These are the heroes. Those without vision, who insist everything stay strictly by some book, become perpetrators of poppycock and are not able to use common sense or creativity when problem solving and exceptions are called for.

A scary thing about human nature is that we will join movements, or stay on certain paths, even when they have taken wrong turns. People become dependent on systems. Although it has become an overused joke topic, a lot of men **and** women don't ask for directions when they are lost. The *intoxication of momentum*, and the unwillingness to backtrack or start over keeps us going forward in all sorts of directions; just not always the right ones. And many don't care because they are only along for the ride. They have no stock in final outcomes but are only concerned with incomes. They don't care which way they go. As long as there's income, that's enough of an outcome. It is this type of system that perpetuates inefficiency, neglect, corruption and greed. For this reason, people with vision are rightfully leery of embracing habits.

To "think outside the box" has become a popular organizational motto. But it is often only superficially embraced. Leaders of organizations can be creative and be thinking originally, then hear some highly effective speaker who inspires them personally. The leaders then return to their organizations and profess to have found some great philosophy that has universal implications and will contribute greatly to their companies' ways of doing business. They feel strongly that they have discovered the correct way to think and behave for the times. The leaders herd their employees, with little regard for or interest in *their* existing thoughts and behaviors, with little regard for *their* creative and original processes, and with very little understanding of what *their* existing way of doing business actually is. The leader has his employees **trained** in this new *new thing*, and the entire organization jumps into another box. Those few original and creative thinkers who are reluctant to jump are viewed with suspicion and contempt and seen as a threat to the new order. And why are they so threatening? Ironically, it may be because they are choosing to stay and think outside the box. Thinking outside the box has to be an ongoing philosophy rather than a short-term goal.

My background is in the following fields: medical/health care, education, entertainment, theatre and music, management and administration, advertising, marketing and speech communication. These fields, if not all fields, are in the human service arena. They require that sixth sense we as human beings possess: the ability to feel what another person is experiencing through our own willingness to be empathic, by giving another enough regard so as to be willing to put ourselves into his or her experience or frame of reference. Nearly all failures in communication, understanding and cooperation come from the lack of willingness to show such regard. Whether a manager, teacher, entertainer, advertiser, medic, administrator, speaker, programmer, nurse, doctor, etc., if one does not connect and feel what his audience or customer or patient or student or employee *needs*, he will not be successful in his functions.

1

Connect

The ache for home lives in all of us, the safe place where we can go as we are and not be questioned.

Maya Angelou

Think of a person you feel a strong connection with. What makes it strong? What specific behaviors are present in both of you that promote such synergy? William Glasser's **CHOICE THEORY** tells us that the best relationships exist where people do not try to control one another using external control techniques, which are dominant throughout the history of mankind. People trying to get people to do what they do not want to do, is the basis for most dysfunction in human existence. This coercion is the negative glue of dysfunctional relationships, families and companies, all over the world.

Now, look at you and your best friend. There's a kind of "just hanging out and enjoying" mentality that feels great, yet a lot of positive growth and activity and successful re-creation evolves from this state of mind. You have a sense of belonging. You have a sense of power that you and your friend can accomplish great things together.

You feel free, and you're having fun, and your motivation is through the roof!

Those you feel a strong connection with who are troubled or ill, cause you to make yourself worry, and you do what you can to help them back to stability, thus restoring your own homeostasis and the positive synergy you enjoy.

Martin Buber's* book **Ich und Du (I and Thou)** describes the dysfunctional and disconnected relationship as an *I and it* relationship. One person sees the other as an "*it*", as merely an object, which is part of a selfish agenda. The *it* person is not to be regarded with any empathy. He is only a thing to manipulate and serve the great and powerful "*I*". The I and Thou relationship is where the *I* sees the other person as an end in him or herself and worthy of total regard, of the same intensity one reflexively reserves for oneself.

* *Ich und Du* (*I and Thou*), Martin Buber (See Recommended Reading List)

Many people have had significantly hurt feelings in their lives because of dysfunctional relationships and have suffered from a loss of belonging. They become wary and find it difficult to re-establish relationships and they detach themselves as a means of self-preservation. From this detachment, it is quite difficult to establish sincere regard for another, and in this state, a person's circle of friends is quite meager.

In work settings, these dispossessed people display a lack of affect and reserve animation for only one or a few "special" cohorts and usually only in specific, private surroundings such as during a break or in a lunch room corner. These cliques become labeled as deviants by those in power, those who feel at ease with their public display of enthusiasm for being at work, and whose demonstrations of such comfort and satisfaction become more and more chastised by the eye-rolling "lost boys" in the corner. The gaps widen. More and more cliques develop. Morale drops. A sense of direction is lost and the team disappears. People begin to reserve their animation for social scenes and their home fires.

My father told me once that if I wanted to get on people's good sides, I should invite them to talk about themselves. My father models extremely good listening skills. He asks questions that demonstrate he is locked on and empathizing with what is being told to him. This is an art. To truly connect with another, one needs to invest the time to demonstrate true regard. To invite people to sit down and tell their story. "Where are you from? Have you been living here long? Do you have a large family? How was your vacation? Where did you go?" And so on. Listen with your active brain. *Paint pictures of what they're describing and put yourself into those pictures.* When we demonstrate such regard for others and show such a willingness to relate, these people become part of us and the regard we have for them becomes strong and natural. Most of our interactions consequently become friendlier and more familiar. And when sorrowful or traumatic experiences find their way to you or these friends, the support comes and lingers with sincerity. The quiet and active listening is there for the one who needs it. And the bond helps the group get through the hard times. With the demonstration of regard comes undeniable connection.

2

Humanize

It is self-evident that if we can't take the risk of saying or doing something wrong, our creativity goes right out the window... The essence of creativity is not the possession of some special talent; it is much more the ability to play.

John Cleese

Human beings make mistakes. We start out willing to explore and investigate new things with curiosity. But as we advance, we attach a huge stigma to mistakes, and in our efforts to prevent them and the stigma attached to them, we significantly limit our scope of experiences. When we at times throw caution to the wind and go out on a limb and are successful and something works out, we say "Yes!" and pump our fists. However, if there is a circle of inquisitive onlookers with concern on their faces, scrutinizing our steps on our way out onto the limb, we most likely will go back and grab the tree.

Books and articles document Edison's and Lincoln's many failures on their ways to success, but they do not delve into the behaviors of the onlookers as deeply as they might. Not everyone has the fortitude of an Abraham Lincoln or a Thomas Edison; thus many of us are easily dissuaded by discouragement, especially if our failure in an enterprise is greeted by chastisement. Chastisement poisons the creative process to such a degree that some people become much more comfortable doing nothing.

I have been at boardroom tables and seen viciousness and open, boisterous ridicule when someone offers up a bad idea. A lot of people absolutely come alive when they have an opportunity to slam something or someone; yet, when someone offers up a good idea, these same people say nothing and respond with blank stares...so much for positive reinforcement. We're just not good at offering support. But we can reflexively spurt out a buzzer sound, render a Bronx cheer, produce a sour face or plug our nose. We denounce with passion. We are good at that.

Have you ever locked your keys in the car? It's hard to surpass such a feeling of helplessness. How should you respond when someone tells you that he or she has just experienced this troublesome, embarrassing mishap? Some choices are: the blank stare, the "way-to-go-you-moron" clap, or the "I've done that before, I know how you feel, and I'll drop everything right now to help you" attitude. Those who choose the third are the people I want to work with. If I am brainstorming and come up with a less than perfect suggestion, I will not be chastised. My suggestion may receive some collaborative criticism, but the manner of the criticism will be aimed at preserving dignity.

In our formative years, we humans can bounce up from our mistakes with joy and laugh at ourselves and try again. As we move forward in our development and become part of supposedly progressed societal circles, the pressure for us flawed beings to project false perfection is immense. In this arena of dishonesty, mistakes do not facilitate learning, but rather are concealed and often do not get fixed. People are afraid of thinking or acting "outside the box" and motivation and freedom to try new ways are left to Edison and Lincoln, and they're dead.

To be tolerant of mistakes in the workplace and home and to value the person greater than the materials he or she affects, are two of the basic principles for the emotionally functional environments that promote creativity and progress.

3

Emote

As long as there's a bit of a laugh going on, things are alright, but as soon as this infernal seriousness raises its head, like an ugly slick, all is lost.

D. H. Lawrence

Work is love made visible. And if you cannot work with love but only distaste, it is better that you should leave your work and sit at the gate of the temple and take alms from those who work with joy.

Kahlil Gibran

When an adult holds a six-month-old baby, and the baby starts to cry, the adult modulates his voice, raises his eyebrows, smiles and assures the baby that he is in good, happy hands. The adult may sing or make cooing noises, and thus connects with the baby in a manner fitting for the child's individual needs. This same intuitive adult will modify his countenance for the sake of connection with a toddler, preschooler, youngster, adolescent or teen. These adaptive mannerisms are employed to create a bond and demonstrate character and concern. Yet, with adults, particularly at work, this same person may project a stiff, jaded demeanor, preventing himself from appearing concerned or possessing any character at all.

I used to work with a woman whose most common display of character was a "You're a jerk and don't ever expect me to be kind to you" demeanor. People laughed and thought she was funny, including myself, most the time. But attempts to break through that façade and find the inner person and the warmth seemed futile. As I continued to befriend her, and listened to her stories and shared some jokes and thought we were progressing to a connection, she would be totally rude again. Once, after seeing me interact with a customer, she made an accusation and pronounced, "Frank, you're just nice to people so you'll get on their good side and they'll like you." I paused and thought for a few seconds and replied, "Yep. You're right!"

Somewhere in our human histories, we have learned that it is not cool to be expressive or outwardly nice to others. People are afraid of being labeled a sycophant—a brown noser, a boot licker, suck up or worse—a butt plug. This cool, *nothing fazes me, been there done that, know everything attitude* begins developing in adolescence when we're trying to belong to the advanced circles of adulthood, and sticks with many of us, because it is so practical in a world where people frequently act that way. I have seen high-school boys and girls simply full of animation at their lockers talking and laughing and hand-slapping. Then, as they separate and become individuals, they walk down the hall expressionless, making eye contact with no one, in some different *coolworld*. If an adult attempts to break the trance even to say hi, they are aghast and will mutter a reply and hurry back into their own model of coolness.

Being "on the clock" should not mean you're guarding Buckingham Palace or the Tomb of the Unknown Soldier. Think about this: clowns take their jobs very seriously and being professional simply means performing at a constant despite distractions. Clowns are full of animation and professional. That is the constant they strive for. What constant should we strive for? I'm not suggesting we exaggerate our expressions as a clown does, but we should be willing to animate ourselves for everyone, for the sake of connection, to whatever degree is appropriate for the individual. We also should not be afraid of expressing kindness. Even when it is misunderstood and labeled as false when it is sincere, the labeling is being done by someone stuck in the *coolworld* paradigm discussed above. Continue with the effort of expressing sincere kindness, and the consistency will pay off. Remember the cardinal rule of behavior modification: "To change another's behavior, first you must change your own." Allowing yourself to show amazement and animation and joy and kindness can create a *realworld*.

4

Recognize

To affect the quality of the day. That is the highest of arts.

Henry David Thoreau

Considering the lack of animation discussed in the last chapter, we can understand that when we *bring the robot* to work, we are not able to show regard for others. We do not recognize them as other people at all. They are just other robots. Sincere recognition is the positive glue of life. When we show our appreciation and gratitude and let others know that something they have done has truly impressed us, our effort is often greeted by discomfort because these things are so rarely offered. It really is something that we would do well to get used to. As an example, say to someone, "I saw you talking with that patient (customer, student, employee...) this morning, and he was hanging on to your every word. You have a real knack for making people feel like they're in good hands. You're very good. They *are* in good hands...". To say that with sincerity, *makes* that person's day, week, and perhaps even their career. You have just reinforced his or her positive action with attention to specifics. You didn't merely say, "Good job." No, you pointed out what you saw with detail and took a moment, planted your feet and delivered some meaningful communication. Many are not comfortable with this scenario. Sadly though, if they have noticed some transgression or misbehavior, they *are* pretty comfortable and willing to schedule a meeting behind closed doors, with witnesses, and put that sort of recognition in writing and into a personnel file.

Giving positive recognition becomes natural when practiced. It is what good people do. Many wouldn't think twice about giving reinforcement to a child with animation, but for peers we reserve instead a lot of sarcastic criticism, ridicule, and teasing, followed up with the, "I was only kidding" line. It is so easy to fall into the trap of becoming a proponent of light cruelty. It's the easiest type of humor and the workplace is full of targets. We focus on quirks, find a colleague with a compatible personality for an audience, and bring up the person and his peculiar difference that sets him apart. It may be acceptable office culture, but is it balanced with positive recognition? Is the positive recognition embraced with the same heightened energy as the light cruelty?

People who are trying to improve their workplaces should explore these areas. They might want to peruse their personnel files and see how many contain documentation of *rightdoing*. Remember the cardinal rule of behavior modification? It is sad that often when an employee is publicly recognized for achievement in front of his or her peers, there is always a group of people stealthily making eye contact and thus projecting their negative spin on what should be a positive moment. Until we *practice* positive recognition, we won't be very good at it.

5

Illegalize Snapping

What irksome constraint I underwent, sitting in the same attitude hours upon hours, afraid to move an arm or a leg lest Miss Murdstone should complain (as she did on the least pretence) of my restlessness, and afraid to move an eye lest she should light on some look of dislike or scrutiny that would find new cause for complaint in mine...a monstrous load that I was obliged to bear, a daymare that there was no possibility of breaking in, a weight that brooded on my wits, and blunted them...what a blank space I seemed, which everybody overlooked, and yet was in everybody's way.

From *David Copperfield*
by Charles Dickens

Displays of frustration and anger evaporate credibility. Although an enlightened individual is tolerant and forgiving of the occasional snapping of human beings, the common busy office of diverse agendas is not, and when someone barks or brings an angry countenance to the workplace, everyone is impacted. If this negativity escalates and some one or group is the target of the hostility, the broken spirit and resentment that follow become wet blankets over whatever creative fires were previously ignited. Cracking the whip breeds resentment. Barking displays a lack of respect. And the result could be an office full of the disheartened, such as the young David Copperfield in the passage above.

I was working in the emergency room of an air base hospital in Germany in the early eighties, when a WWII veteran, who was visiting his grandson, an active duty air force pilot, came in with rectal bleeding. The emergency room physician that day, a surgeon with a bark, instructed me to prepare the patient for a procto.

This procedure entails laying the disrobed patient on his stomach and elevating the table, and bending the table in the center, so the patient is bent over, upside down. With this gentleman thus positioned, and covered with a blanket, we waited and waited. After ten minutes I assertively called the doctor on the phone and told him the patient was prepped and positioned for the procedure. He was writing notes in the medical library, and in a not-so-kind tone, said he would be right down. I conversed with the patient and explained it would be a while. He was apprehensive and in some discomfort with some abdominal cramping and feeling a bit lightheaded from being in the position he was in. We continued to wait for fifteen minutes more and the doctor still had not arrived. I was really feeling bad for this patient so I lowered and flattened the table. Ten minutes later the doctor brusquely entered, rudely admonished me for not having the patient in the proper position, readjusted the table and essentially shoved a gloved finger up this man, while asking how long he had been noticing the bleeding. He never greeted this man nor attempted to ease his mind at all. I moved to the patient's head and laid my hand on his shoulder and told him it wouldn't be much longer, when the doctor snapped, "Come here and look at this!" The frightened man asked what had been discovered, and the doctor almost joyously announced that he had a ruptured vein that would need to be repaired. I wonder how a person becomes so calloused and oblivious to human needs.

How differently that entire scenario could have been if we had treated the man as a *thou*, and regarded him with the utmost and deserved respect. I took action against that physician by reporting his demeanor to the hospital commander. I wish I could say that his manner improved, but if anything, especially toward me, his behavior worsened.

I was a twenty-two year old senior airman at the time. He was a full-bird colonel. How dare I presume to recommend improvements in patient care to him?

This inhuman incident was a grave abuse of power. Unfortunately, similar but less serious incidents occur often in our workplaces. We all from time to time go about our individual routines and use less diplomacy than we could. We may abruptly have a *Just Do It* manner with our colleagues. It may be we are only modeling what we have been exposed to throughout our varied careers, and it has become second nature to us. But, one only has to be on the receiving end of this type of behavior once to feel its effect, and this should serve as reason enough to avoid it as much as possible.

Managing our relationships with one another takes practice. We practice because we care. If we don't care, we need to learn to care, and that too, takes practice.

6

Harmonize

A master in the art of living knows no sharp distinction between his work and his play, his labor and his leisure, his mind and his body, his education and his recreation. He hardly knows which is which. He simply pursues his vision of excellence through whatever he is doing and leaves others to determine whether he is working or playing. To himself he always seems to be doing both.

George Bernard Shaw

In Springfield, Oregon my wife and I stopped at a diner for breakfast one morning. There were two women waiting on tables and another helping at the cash register. The woman at the register smiled as we entered and asked, "Two for breakfast?" We smiled back and said yes. We were close to our son's house in Eugene, after driving for the past seven days, and glad to be done with the final western leg of our trip. She walked us over to our table and asked us if we wanted coffee. We told her we did. She got it and came back, gave us our menus and told us our waitress would be right over. From the kitchen, we heard a woman's voice say, "Debbie, Hon!" Another waitress in the dining area replied, "Thanks, Hon!" Then our waitress came over and served us with the same exuberant warmth. "Sheila, Hon!" came out of the kitchen. Our waitress answered, "Thanks, Hon!" and went to pick up another order. I looked around the dining area. There were probably thirty patrons, and no one was waiting long.

The harmony in this establishment was a direct result of the people working there. Calling each other "Hon" added to the contagious affection that prevailed at our breakfast that morning. (Our waitress asked where we were from. When we told her New York, she asked why we weren't yelling at her.) Henry David Thoreau said, "To affect the quality of the day. That is the highest of arts." Each of us does indeed have the tools to contribute a positive force to whatever environment we are occupying.

Each of us knows we could say something or not say something or do something or not do something and cause someone to have a rotten moment or day. I have asked my audiences, "Who thinks they have the ability to ruin somebody's day if they want to?" The exuberance of the hand raising is amazing. When I ask if they think they have the ability to *make* someone's day, they almost always reply with a matter-of-fact, "Yeah, probably."

Despite our differences, with enough willingness to open ourselves to a constant awareness to each other's needs, and a focus on **connecting, humanizing, emoting,** and **recognizing**, we can affect the quality of our days. If we do **illegalize snapping,** then the **harmonizing** will come naturally, and like this Springfield diner, we will create a con-cert of warmth for all to enjoy, Hon.

Conclusion

One hundred people sitting in a room will agree that none of them has ever had a perfectly identical experience. One hundred people will agree that if they were each to grab a set of identical directions for the assembly of a child's tricycle, each of them would vary in the methods they use to complete the task. So isn't it remarkable that just about everyone in the world tries to get others to do things their way?

Whether it is which road to take, or what hotel to stay in, or where to eat, or how to prepare a meal, each of us likes to influence or perhaps even control those around us. Maybe it's simply an urge to share common experiences and feel a bond, or pass on traditions. Or perhaps, it's to leave our own mark on as many experiences as possible, whether they're our own, or not. Of course, there are always times when someone can lend his or her experience to guide someone along and help them save time or prevent disaster, but the style of the lending is paramount. We need to take care to promote participation and some ownership, and prevent losing an opportunity for the discovery of ingenuity and dignity. Regardless, allowing people around us to have individual preferences, or to figure out something on their own, or create a new way of doing something, interferes with the learned and ingrained parent-teacher-boss in all of us. Yet, having the freedom to make our own choices, to be creative and to solve problems on our own, is something most of us embrace. And when we do make our own choices, and create new methods, and solve problems on our own, we take pride. We have learned. We seek credit. We have learned how to do something new. And guess what? It's time to show somebody else...

In his book CHOICE THEORY, William Glasser discusses human needs for belonging, freedom, power, and fun. In human dynamics, the strongest bonds are forged by good people who allow others to learn, create and figure things out on their own. Then, they *also* permit them to show what they know with encouragement and delight, and without interference or an "of course I already knew that" attitude. The encouragement and delight is not insincere; it results from recognition of the person's discovery, and the knowledge that his or her newly found ability will have its own individual traits. Being empowering takes leadership and true regard for others. Freedom and power often result from others simply allowing people to be.

When one feels empowerment and freedom, energy levels soar and the chances for creative brilliance are abundant. However, when one feels scrutinized by a cynic who projects the *been there, done that, you can't show me anything I don't already know* attitude, his or her motivation is gone. I believe people prefer to feel empowered and free, and if I can project an empowering attitude, motivated and creative people will surround me. If I project the *nothing surprises me* stance, no one around me will ever feel much motivation to create anything, and our day to day experiences will remain predictably bland.

We all have the innate abilities to mold our environments into places of tolerance, regard and respect. With these attributes, we feel belonging and empowerment, and our workplaces evolve into extensions, rather than disruptions, of our lives.

Recommended Readings

Buber, Martin, *Ich und Du (I and Thou)*, New York: Scribner, 1970 (First Edition 1936)

Cloke, Kenneth & Goldsmith, Joan, *Thank God It's Monday! 14 Values We Need to Humanize the Way We Work*, Chicago: Irwin Professional Publishing, 1997

Freiberg, Kevin & Jackie, *NUTS! Southwest Airlines' Crazy Recipe for Business and Personal Success*, New York: Broadway Books, 1996

Glasser, William, M.D., *Choice Theory: A New Psychology of Personal Freedom*, New York: Harper Collins, 1998

Shrock, Dean, Ph.D., *Doctor's Orders: Go Fishing*, State College, PA: First Publishers Group, Ltd., 2000

About the Author

Frank Pastizzo presents dynamic workshops and keynote addresses helping people recognize their own abilities to contribute to the attitude of the workplace. He draws on his experiences as an  emergency room technician, paramedic, child development specialist, high school drama and English teacher, actor, comedian, musician, program manager, administrator and marketing executive. He and his wife, Susan, live in the Adirondack Mountains of New York State in the village of Saranac Lake. To find out more about his presentations, visit his website:

www.warmuptheworkplace.com